EVERS' STANDARD CUT GLASS VALUE GUIDE

Jo Evers

COLLECTOR BOOKS

A Division of Schroeder Publishing Co., Inc.

The current values in this book should be used only as a guide. They are not intended to set prices, which vary from one section of the country to another. Auction prices as well as dealer prices vary greatly and are affected by condition as well as demand. Neither the Author nor the Publisher assumes responsibility for any losses that might be incurred as a result of consulting this guide.

On the Cover:
Clockwise from top:
Two piece punch set, signed Clark, $2,200.00 – 2,500.00
Berry bowl, signed Libby, $175.00 – 200.00
Rose bowl, signed Hawkes, $80.00 – 100.00
Bread tray, signed Clark, $200.00 – 250.00
Jewel box, signed Hoare & Co. Corning (No. 853), $200.00 – 250.00
Berry bowl, signed Hawkes, $125.00 – 150.00
In Center:
Water goblet, signed Hawkes, $80.00 – 100.00
Water carafe, signed Hawkes, $75.00 – 100.00

Searching For A Publisher?

We are always looking for knowledgeable people considered to be experts within their fields. If you feel that there is a real need for a book on your collectible subject and have a large comprehensive collection contact Collector Books.

Additional copies of this book may be ordered from:

COLLECTOR BOOKS
P.O. Box 3009
Paducah, Kentucky 42002-3009

@$12.95. Add $2.00 for postage and handling.

Copyright: Schroeder's Publishing Co. 1975
Values Updated, 1995

Printed by IMAGE GRAPHICS, INC., Paducah, Kentucky

INTRODUCTION

This <u>Standard Cut Glass Value Guide</u> shows nearly 2000 pieces of cut glass from several of the leading distributors and manufacturers during the Brilliant Age (1875–1915.) Not only do we show the current value with each piece of glass illustrated but also the company, pattern, and sizes as well. Since many of the nearly 2,000 pieces were made in several sizes, this book contains some 2,300 current values, making it a guide to treasure for both the collector and dealer alike.

DEFINITION OF CUT GLASS

Cut glass can be defined as a glass having a high lead content that has been hand blown and hand decorated with an abrasive wheel. There were as many as five steps in decorating the glass. From the time the design was sketched on the glass to the polishing and buffing, many man hours were exhausted on a large piece. Toward the end of the Brilliant Period, labor-saving steps were introduced into the industry. These steps ultimately led to near cut and press cut glass that so many today confuse with true cut glass.

SIGNED CUT GLASS

A piece of cut glass with the company logo or trademark etched on it is called "signed glass" and usually commands a premium on today's market. The signature was usually applied with a stamp saturated with an acid solution. Look for a small insignificant trademark with a gray cast. The signature, normally, will be found centered in the inside or outside bottom surface. Some handled pieces are signed on the upper portion of the handle. There are exceptions as to the location of signatures which can be found in most any position on the glass.

PRICING

The prices in this catalog are for near perfect to perfect pieces of cut crystal. It is, of course, extremely difficult to find a piece of mint perfect cut glass today. Small, minute, rim and edge chips can be found on most any piece. Cracked or badly damaged pieces of cut glass are, for all practical purposes, worthless on today's market. Look for cracks, in good light in the deep cut seams, carefully turning at different angles to expose the flaw. Edge and rim chips can be felt as well as seen by the experienced cut glass collector. Finding flaws in cut glass is probably more difficult than any other type of glass because of the many cuts, edges, and facets. "Let the buyer beware." The prices in this book are to be used only as a guide. We have used recent sales catalogs, auction reports, show prices, and dealer values to arrive at a retail value.

CONTENTS

•

BASKETS, HANDLED

Pitkins & Brooks
PANSY BASKET,
ENGRAVED
P & B Grade
8"… $400.00 – 450.00

Pitkins & Brooks
DAISY HANDLED
BASKET, ENGRAVED
P & B Grade
8"…$425.00 – 475.00

Pitkins & Brooks
ELDORADO HANDLED
BASKET
Standard Grade
6"…$350.00 – 400.00

Pitkins & Brooks
SUNBEAM HANDLED
BASKET
P & B Grade
7½"…$200.00 – 250.00

Pitkins & Brooks
ELDORADO HANDLED
BASKET
Standard Grade
6"…$150.00 – 200.00
8"…$300.00 – 350.00

Pitkins & Brooks
OSBORNE HANDLED
BASKET
P & B Grade
6"…$150.00 – 200.00

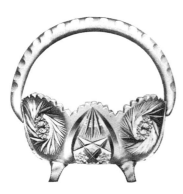

Pitkins & Brooks
ZESTA BASKET
P & B Grade
handled & footed
8"…$350.00 – 400.00

Pitkins & Brooks
ZESTA HANDLED
BASKET
P & B Grade
7"…$200.00 – 250.00

BELLS

T. B, Clark & Co.
BELLS, JEWEL
Large size …$250.00 – 300.00
Small…$200.00 – 250.00

Pitkins & Brooks
DEAN CALL BELL
P & B Grade
5½"…$150.00 – 200.00

CALL BELL
5½"…$250.00 – 300.00

TEA BELL
5½"…$200.00 – 250.00

TEA BELL
5½"…$150.00 – 200.00

J. D. Bergen
PREMIER
6" bell…$150.00 – 200.00
7" bell…$200.00 – 250.00

CALL BELL
Buzz Star Cutting
Each…$175.00 – 225.00

BONBONS

J. D. Bergen
EMBLEM
Olive or
Bonbon...$50.00 – 65.00

J. D. Bergen
EVELYN
Olive or Bonbon
6"...$50.00 – 65.00

J. D. Bergen
BEDFORD
Olive or Bonbon
7"...$60.00 – 75.00

Pitkins & Brooks
HALLE BONBON
P & B Grade
6"...$50.00 – 65.00

Pitkins & Brooks
BEVERLY
P & B Grade
6"...$60.00 – 75.00

Pitkins & Brooks
ORIOLE
Standard Grade
6"...$50.00 – 65.00

Pitkins & Brooks
RAJAH BONBON
P & B Grade
6¾"...$75.00 – 90.00
Standard Grade
6¾"...$50.00 – 65.00

Pitkins & Brooks
MYRTLE BONBON
Standard Grade
7½"...$45.00 – 60.00

Pitkins & Brooks
MARS BONBON
P & B Grade
3½"...$40.00 – 50.00
Standard Grade
3½"...$30.00 – 40.00

Pitkins & Brooks
RAJAH BONBON
P & B Grade
7¼"...$90.00 – 110.00

Higgins & Seiter
WEBSTER
Salted Almond Dish
6"...$40.00 – 50.00

Higgins & Seiter
WALTER SCOTT
Olive or Bonbon,
Heart Shape
5"...$40.00 – 55.00

T. B. Clark & Co.
ARBUTUS
Bonbon
Each...$35.00 – 50.00

BONBONS

J. D. Bergen
DARIEL
Olive or Bonbon
5" x 9"...$90.00 – 110.00

J. D. Bergen
MAGNET
Olive or Bonbon
8"...$50.00 – 65.00

J. D. Bergen
THELMA
Olive or Bonbon
9"...$60.00 – 75.00

J. D. Bergen
HAWTHORNE
Olive or Bonbon
5" x 9"...$120.00 – 150.00

J.D. Bergen
LAUREL
Olive or Bonbon
7"...$55.00 – 70.00

Pitkins & Brooks
DELMAR COVERED
Bonbon
P & B Grade
10"...$250.00 – 300.00

J.D. Bergen
ARGO
Olive or Bonbon
7"...$55.00 – 70.00

Averbeck
DIAMOND
Each...$50.00 – 65.00

Pitkins & Brooks
GARLAND COVERED
BONbON
4"...$40.00 – 50.00
5"...$60.00 – 70.00
6"...$90.00 - 100.00

BONBONS

T. B. Clark & Co.
MANHATTAN
Bonbon
Each…$60.00 – 75.00

T. B. Clark & Co.
MANHATTAN
Bonbon
Each…$60.00 – 75.00

T. B. Clark & Co.
ST. GEORGE
Each…$55.00 – 70.00

Higgins & Seiter
WALTER SCOTT
Olive or Bonbon
5½"…$30.00 –40.00

T. B. Clark & Co.
BONBON, JEWEL
Each…$50.00 – 65.00

T. B. Clark & Co.
BONBON, ADONIS
Each…$60.00 – 75.00

T. B. Clark & Co.
BONBON ST. GEORGE
Each…$50.00 –60.00

Higgins & Seiter
NAPOLEON
Ice Cream, Olive, or
Bonbon
6"…$30.00 – 40.00

Higgins & Seiter
WALTER SCOTT
Olive or Bonbon
6"…$45.00 – 60.00

T. B. Clark
DORRANCE
Bonbon
Each…$60.00 – 75.00

T. B. Clark
WINOLA
Bonbon
Each…$40.00 – 50.00

Higgins & Seiter
ARLINGTON
Handled Bonbon
6"…$35.00 – 50.00

Higgins & Seiter
ARLINGTON
Saucer or Bonbon
5"…$30.00 – 40.00
6"…$40.00 – 50.00

Higgins & Seiter
WALTER SCOTT
Oblong Olive, Pickle,
or Bonbon
4" x 7"…$60.00 – 75.00

T. B. Clark & Co.
BONBON, JEWEL
Each…$40.00 – 50.00

T. B. Clark & Co.
ST. GEORGE
Rd. Handled Bonbon
5"…$30.00 – 40.00
6"…$35.00 – 50.00

T. B. Clark & Co.
IRVING
Handled Bonbon
5"…$60.00 – 65.00
6"…$75.00 – 85.00

T. B. Clark & Co.
JEFFERSON
Handled Bonbon
5" …$50.00 – 65.00
6"…$75.00 – 85.00

BONBONS

Pitkins & Brooks
EARL BONBON
P & B Grade
5½"...$75.00 – 90.00
Standard Grade
5½"...$50.00 – 65.00

Averbeck
LADY CURZON
Each...$70.00 – 85.00

Averbeck
PUCK
Each...$60.00 – 75.00

Pitkins & Brooks
NELLORE BONBON
Standard Grade
5½"...$40.00 – 55.00

Pitkins & Brooks
MARS BONBON
P & B Grade
6¾"...$70.00 – 85.00

Averbeck
SARATOGA
Each...$50.00 – 65.00

Averbeck
AMERICAN BEAUTY
5"...$70.00 – 90.00
6"...$100.00 – 125.00

Averbeck
RUBY
5"...$45.00 – 60.00
6"...$60.00 – 75.00

Pitkins & Brooks
ERMINIE BONBON
P & B Grade
6"...$60.00 – 75.00
Standard Grade
6"...$40.00 – 50.00

Pitkins & Brooks
PLYMOUTH
BONBON
P & B Grade
Each...$125.00 – 150.00

Pitkins & Brooks
STEUBEN BONBON
P & B Grade
5¼"...$35.00 – 45.00
Standard...$25.00 – 35.00

Pitkins & Brooks
ERIC BONBON
P & B Grade
6"...$60.00 – 75.00
Standard Grade
6"...$40.00 – 55.00

Averbeck
RUBY
Each...$45.00 – 60.00

Higgins & Seiter
WALTER SCOTT
Oblong Olive, Pickle,
or Bonbon
4" x 8"...$50.00 – 65.00

Higgins & Seiter
WALTER SCOTT
Olive or Bonbon
Each...$45.00 – 60.00

BONBONS

J. D. Bergen
KEY WEST
Olive or Bonbon
6"…$75.00 – 90.00

Pitkins & Brooks
HIAWATHA BOAT
BONBON
P & B Grade
9"…$50.00 – 60.00

Averbeck
NICE
Each…$75.00 – 90.00

Pitkins & Brooks
OAK LEAF
BONBON
P & B Grade
5½"…$75.00 – 90.00

Averbeck
PARIS
Each…$75.00 – 90.00

Pitkins & Brooks
PRINCE
P & B Grade
6"…$60.00 – 75.00

Pitkins & Brooks
OSBORNE BONBON
P & B Grade
7"…$75.00 – 90.00

Averbeck
DIAMOND
Each…$75.00 – 90.00

Averbeck
AMERICAN BEAUTY
5"…$60.00 – 75.00
6"…$75.00 – 90.00

Pitkins & Brooks
ESTHER BONBON
Standard Grade
3¼"…$50.00 – 60.00

Averbeck
NAPLES
Each…$75.00 – 90.00

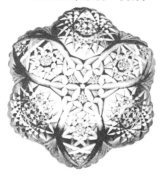

Averbeck
MARIETTA
EACH…$75.00 – 90.00

Pitkins & Brooks
CRESCENT BONBON
P & B GRADE
4¾"…$40.00 – 55.00

Pitkins & Brooks
MYRTLE BONBON
P & B Grade
4¾"…$40.00 – 55.00

Pitkins & Brooks
PINTO BONBON
P & B Grade
6"…$85.00 – 100.00
7"…$100.00 – 125.00

BONBONS

J. D. Bergen
RIPPLE
Olive or Bonbon
6"...$75.00 – 90.00

Averbeck
FLEUR DE LIS
Each...$75.00 – 90.00

J. D. Bergen
BRIGHTON
Olive or Bonbon
7"...$75.00 – 90.00

Averbeck
PUCK
Each...$75.00 – 90.00

Averbeck
DIAMOND
Each...$75.00 – 90.00

Averbeck
RUBY
5"...$55.00 – 70.00
6"...$75.00 – 90.00

Averbeck
SARATOGA
Each...$65.00 – 80.00

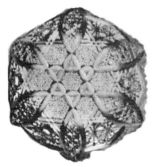

Averbeck
AMERICAN BEAUTY
Each...$100.00 – 125.00

Averbeck
AMERICAN BEAUTY
5"...$65.00 – 80.00
6"...$110.00 – 125.00

Pitkins & Brooks
PIZO BONBON
P & B Grade
7"...$100.00 – 125.00

Pitkins & Brooks
HEART BONBON
P & B Grade
5½"...$$75.00 – 90.00
Standard Grade
5½"...$45.00 – 60.00

J. D. Bergen
PILGRIM
Bonbon
6"...$100.00 – 125.00

J.D. Bergen
DIADEM
Bonbon or Spoon Tray
8"...$85.00 – 100.00

J. D. Bergen
EMBLEM
Olive or Bonbon
Each...$75.00 – 90.00

BONBONS

J. D. Bergen
MAGNET
Olive or Bonbon
6½"...$60.00 – 75.00

Pitkins & Brooks
RAJAH BONBON
P & B Grade
7½"...$75.00 – 90.00

J. D. Bergen
JUNO
Olive or Bonbon
7"...$65.00 – 80.00

J. D. Bergen
RUTH
Olive or Bonbon
4" x 6½"...$65.00 – 80.00
5" x 7"...$90.00 – 100.00

T. B. Clark & Co.
BONBON, JEWEL
Each...$35.00 – 50.00

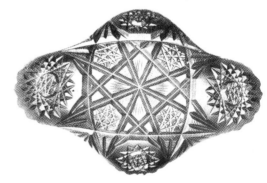

J. D. Bergen
MADISON
Bonbon or Spoon Tray
8"...$85.00 – 100.00

J. D. Bergen
CAPRICE
Olive or Bonbon
7"...$75.00 – 90.00

Pitkins & Brooks
MEADVILLE
Bonbon
Standard Grade
7"...$50.00 – 65.00

J. D. Bergen
MAGNET
Olive or Bonbon
7½"...$75.00 – 90.00

J. D. Bergen
KEYSTONE
Olive or Bonbon
7"...$75.00 – 90.00

Pitkins & Brooks
MEADVILLE
Bonbon
Standard Grade
6½"...$40.00 – 50.00

J. D. Bergen
LAUREL
Olive or Bonbon
7"...$75.00 – 90.00

BOWLS

Higgins & Seiter
FLORIDA
Fruit or Berry Bowl
9¼" x 13½"...$135.00 – 155.00

T. B. Clark & Co.
MANHATTAN
Priscilla Bowls
8"...$150.00 – 200.00
9"...$200.00 – 250.00

Higgins & Seiter
TORNADO
Nappie, Low Fruit,
Salad, or Berry Bowl
8"...$105.00 – 120.00
9"...$120.00 – 135.00
10"...$135.00 – 150.00

Higgins & Seiter
MONARCH
Cut Glass Bowl
8"...$75.00 – 100.00
9"...$100.00 – 125.00
10"...$150.00 – 200.00

Higgins & Seiter
JUBILEE
Rich Cut Glass Bowl
8"...$75.00 – 100.00
9"...$100.00 – 125.00
10"...$150.00 – 200.00

Higgins & Seiter
WEBSTER
Nut, Fruit, or Berry Bowl
8"...$65.00 – 90.00
9"...$90.00 – 115.00
10"...$115.00 – 150.00

T. B. Clark & Co.
ARBUTUS
7"...$60.00 – 75.00
8"...$75.00 – 95.00
9"...$95.00 – 120.00
10"...$125.00 – 150.00

Pitkins & Brooks
MARS FANCY BOWL
P & B Grade
9½"...$150.00 – 200.00

T. B. Clark & Co.
DESDEMONA
8"...$75.00 – 100.00
9"...$100.00 – 125.00
10"...$150.00 – 200.00
12"...$275.00 – 325.00

Pitkins & Brooks
VENICE SALAD BOWL
P & B Grade
8"...$75.00 – 100.00
9"...$100.00 -125.00

Pitkins & Brooks
MYRTLE SALAD BOWL
Standard Grade
8"...$65.00 – 80.00

Pitkins & Brooks
MEADVILLE SALAD
BOWL
Standard Grade
8"...$65.00 – 80.00
9"...$80.00 – 100.00

15

BOWLS

T. B. Clark & Co.
PRISCILLA – ORIENT
7"...$150.00 – 200.00
8"...$200.00 – 250.00
9"...$300.00 – 350.00

T. B. Clark & Co.
MANHATTAN
7"...$75.00 – 100.00
8"...$125.00 – 150.00
9"...$150.00 – 175.00
10"...$175.00 – 200.00

T. B. Clark & Co.
VENUS
8"...$125.00 – 175.00
9"...$200.00 – 250.00
10"...$250.00 – 300.00

T. B. Clark & Co.
ADONIS
9"...$150.00 – 200.00

T. B. Clark & Co.
WINOLA
7"...$75.00 – 100.00
8"...$125.00 – 150.00
9"...$150.00 – 175.00

T. B. Clark & Co.
DESDEMONA
9"...$200.00 – 225.00

Higgins & Seiter
8"...$100.00 – 125.00
9"...$125.00 – 150.00
10"...$125.00 – 150.00

Higgins & Seiter
GLEN
Nappie or Berry Bowl
8"...$70.00 – 80.00
9"...$90.00 – 110.00
10"...$125.00 – 150.00

T. B. Clark & Co.
ADONIS
7"...$100.00 – 120.00
8"...$125.00 – 150.00
9"...$150.00 – 200.00
10"...$200.00 – 250.00

Higgins & Seiter
ARLINGTON
8"...$70.00 – 80.00
9"...$90.00 – 110.00
10"...$125.00 – 150.00

T. B. Clark & Co.
VENUS
8"...$125.00 – 175.00
9"...$200.00 – 250.00
10"...$250.00 – 300.00
12"...$300.00 – 350.00

T. B. Clark & Co.
ARBUTUS
8"...$70.00 – 80.00
9"...$90.00 – 110.00
10"...$125.00 –150.00

BOWLS

Pitkins & Brooks
MIKADO SALAD BOWL
P & B Grade
8"…$80.00 – 100.00

Pitkins & Brooks
DUCHESS SALAD
BOWL
P & B GRADE
8"…$135.00 – 160.00

Pitkins & Brooks
CARNEGIE SALAD
BOWL
P & B Grade
8"…$80.00 – 100.00

Pitkins & Brooks
RAJAH FANCY BOWL
P & B Grade
8"…$150.00 – 175.00

Pitkins & Brooks
NELLORE SALAD
BOWL
P & B Grade
8"…$80.00 – 100.00

Pitkins & Brooks
LYRE SALAD BOWL
Standard Grade
8"…$70.00 – 80.00

Pitkins & Brooks
ORIOLE FANCY
BOWL – OVAL
P & B Grade
10"…$135.00 –150.00

Averbeck
ACME BOWL
7"…$75.00 –100.00
8"…$125.00 – 150.00
9"…$150.00 – 175.00
10"…$175.00 – 200.00

Pitkins & Brooks
VENICE SALAD BOWL
P & B Grade
8"…$80.00 – 100.00
9"…$100.00 – 125.00

Averbeck
OCCIDENT BOWL
7"…$100.00 – 125.00
8"…$150.00 – 175.00
9"…$200.00 – 225.00
10"…$250.00 – 300.00

Averbeck
WEBSTER
Fruit, Salad, or Berry
8"…$80.00 – 100.00
9"..$100.00 – 125.00
10"…$125.00 – 150.00

Higgins & Seiter
MONARCH
Nappie
8"…$60.00 – 75.00
9"…$75.00 – 90.00
10"…$90.00 – 110.00

T. B. Clark & Co.
MANHATTAN
7"…$75.00 – 100.00
8"…$125.00 – 150.00
9"…$150.00 – 175.00
10"…$175.00 – 200.00
12"…$200.00 – 250.00

Higgins & Seiter
8"…$100.00 – 125.00
9"…$125.00 – 150.00
10"…$150.00 – 175.00

T. B. Clark & Co.
CARNATION
8"…$125.00 – 150.00
9"…$150.00 – 175.00
10"…$175.00 – 225.00

Higgins & Seiter
TORNADO
8"…$125.00 – 150.00
9"…$150.00 – 200.00

Higgins & Seiter
CORONET
8"…$80.00 – 90.00

Higgins & Seiter
PEERLESS
Salad, Fruit, or
Berry Bowl with Tray
Each…$250.00 – 300.00

T. B. Clark & Co.
DESDEMONA
Each…$200.00 – 225.00

T. B. Clark & Co.
PALMETTO
9"…$200.00 – 225.00

T. B. Clark & Co.
ADONIS
Each…$100.00 – 250.00

Higgins & Seiter
LISBON
8"…$70.00 – 80.00

T. B. Clark & Co.
MAGNOLIA
8"…$100.00 – 125.00
9"…$125.00 – 150.00
10"…$150.00 – 200.00

Higgins & Seiter
WEBSTER
Fruit, Salad, or Berry
8"…$80.00 – 100.00
9"…$100.00 – 125.00
10"…$125.00 – 150.00

BOWLS

Pitkins & Brooks
CORSAIR SALAD
BOWL
Standard Grade
8"...$60.00 – 75.00
9"...$75.00 – 100.00

Averbeck
MARIETTA BOWL
7"...$65.00 – 75.00
8"...$75.00 – 90.00
9"...$90.00 – 110.00
10"...$125.00 – 150.00

Pitkins & Brooks
WINONA SALAD
BOWL
P & B Grade
8"...$100.00 – 125.00
9"...$125.00 – 150.00

Averbeck
LIBERTY BOWL
7"...$65.00 – 80.00
8"...$80.00 – 95.00
9"...$100.00 – 125.00
10"...$150.00 – 200.00

Averbeck
GEORGIA BOWL
8"...$80.00 – 95.00
9"...$100.00 – 125.00
10"...$150.00 – 200.00

Averbeck
AMERICAN BEAUTY
BOWL
7"...$60.00 – 75.00
8"...$85.00 – 110.00
9"...$125.00 –150.00
10"...$175.00 –225.00

Pitkins & Brooks
CLARION SALAD
BOWL
P & B Grade
7"...$90.00 – 100.00

Averbeck
HUDSON BOWL
7"...$65.00 – 80.00
8"...$80.00 – 95.00
9"...$100.00 –125.00
10"...$150.00 – 200.00

Pitkins & Brooks
RAJAH SALAD BOWL
P & B Grade
8"...$150.00 – 175.00
9"...$175.00 – 200.00
10"...$200.00 – 250.00

Pitkins & Brooks
ELSIE SALAD BOWL
P & B Grade
8"...$100.00 – 125.00

Averbeck
RUBY BOWL
7"...$65.00 – 80.00
8"...$80.00 – 90.00
9"...$100.00 – 125.00
10"...$150.00 – 200.00

Averbeck
CAIRO BOWL
9"...$150.00 – 200.00

Averbeck
LONDON
Oval Bowl or Dish
10"...$175.00 – 225.00

Averbeck
SPRUCE BOWL
7"...$60.00 – 75.00
8"...$75.00 – 90.00
9"...$90.00 – 110.00
10"...$120.00 – 150.00

Pitkins & Brooks
MARS SALAD BOWL
P & B Grade
8"...$125.00 – 150.00
9"...$150.00 – 200.00

BOWLS

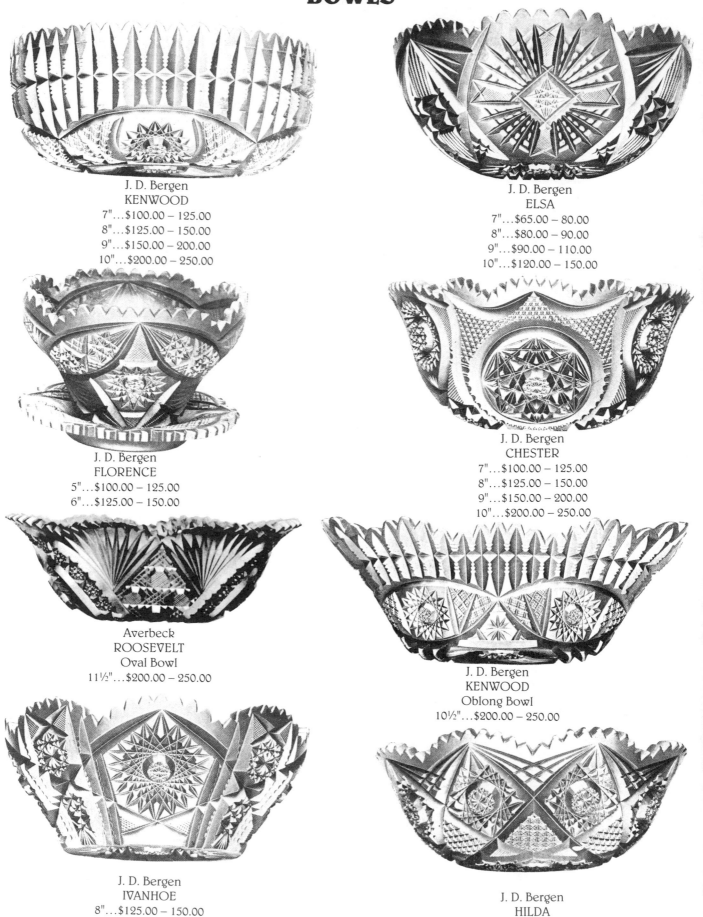

J. D. Bergen
KENWOOD
7"...$100.00 – 125.00
8"...$125.00 – 150.00
9"...$150.00 – 200.00
10"...$200.00 – 250.00

J. D. Bergen
ELSA
7"...$65.00 – 80.00
8"...$80.00 – 90.00
9"...$90.00 – 110.00
10"...$120.00 – 150.00

J. D. Bergen
FLORENCE
5"...$100.00 – 125.00
6"...$125.00 – 150.00

J. D. Bergen
CHESTER
7"...$100.00 – 125.00
8"...$125.00 – 150.00
9"...$150.00 – 200.00
10"...$200.00 – 250.00

Averbeck
ROOSEVELT
Oval Bowl
11½"...$200.00 – 250.00

J. D. Bergen
KENWOOD
Oblong Bowl
10½"...$200.00 – 250.00

J. D. Bergen
IVANHOE
8"...$125.00 – 150.00
9"...$150.00 – 200.00

J. D. Bergen
HILDA
8"...$125.00 – 150.00

BOWLS

J. D. Bergen
AMBROSE
7"…$100.00 – 125.00
8"…$125.00 – 150.00
9"…$150.00 – 200.00
10"…$200.00 – 250.00

J. D. Bergen
GOLF
7"…$65.00 – 80.00
8"…$80.00 – 90.00
9"…$90.00 –110.00
10"…$125.00 – 150.00

J. D. Bergen
RENWICK
7"…$100.00 – 125.00
8"…$125.00 – 150.00
9"…$150.00 – 200.00
10"…$200.00 – 250.00

J. D. Bergen
HAMPTON
7"…$100.00 – 125.00
8"…$125.00 – 150.00
9"…$150.00 – 200.00
10"…$200.00 – 250.00

J. D. Bergen
BERMUDA
7"…$65.00 – 80.00
8"…$80.00 – 100.00
9"…$100.00 – 125.00
10"…$135.00 – 160.00

J. D. Bergen
GOLDENROD
7"…$65.00 – 80.00
8"…$80.00 – 100.00
9"…$100.00 – 125.00
10"…$135.00 – 160.00

BOWLS

J. D. Bergen
MARLOW
7"...$65.00 – 80.00
8"...$80.00 – 100.00
9"...$100.00 – 130.00
10"...$150.00 – 175.00

J. D. Bergen
ST. LOUIS
7"...$65.00 – 80.00
8"...$80.00 – 100.00
9"...$100.00 – 130.00
10"...$150.00 – 175.00

J. D. Bergen
CORSAIR
7"...$65.00 – 80.00
8"...$80.00 – 100.00
9"...$100.00 – 130.00
10"...$150.00 – 175.00

J. D. Bergen
WEBSTER
7"...$65.00 – 80.00
8"...$80.00 – 100.00
9"...$100.00 – 130.00
10"...$150.00 – 175.00

J. D. Bergen
KEYSTONE
7"...$60.00 – 75.00
8"...$75.00 – 95.00
9"...$100.00 – 120.00
10"...$125.00 – 150.00

J. D. Bergen
BEDFORD
7"...$65.00 – 80.00
8"...$80.00 – 100.00
9"...$100.00 – 130.00
10"...$150.00 – 175.00

BOWLS

Averbeck
CANTON BOWL
7"…$60.00 – 75.00
8"…$75.00 – 90.00
9"…$90.00 – 110.00
10"…$120.00 – 150.00

J. D. Bergen
MAGNET
7"…$50.00 – 65.00
8"…$75.00 – 90.00

Averbeck
NICE BOWL
7"…$65.00 – 80.00
8"…$80.00 – 100.00
9"…$100.00 – 130.00
10"…$150.00 – 175.00

Averbeck
DAISY BOWL
7"…$100.00 – 125.00
8"…$125.00 – 150.00
9"…$150.00 – 200.00
10"…$200.00 – 250.00

Pitkins & Brooks
CLEO SALAD BOWL
P & B Grade
8"…$125.00 – 150.00

Averbeck
FRISCO BOWL
8"…$75.00 – 90.00
9"…$90.00 – 110.00
10"…$120.00 – 150.00

Averbeck
GENOA
Oval Bowl or Dish
10"…$200.00 – 250.00

MONARCH
8"…$80.00 – 100.00
9"…$100.00 – 130.00
10"…$150.00 – 175.00

Pitkins & Brooks
PINTO DISH
P & B Grade
10"…$150.00 – 175.00

Averbeck
PUCK BOWL
8"…$75.00 – 90.00
9"…$90.00 – 110.00
10"…$120.00 – 150.00

Averbeck
DIAMOND BOWL
7"…$100.00 – 125.00
8"…$125.00 – 150.00
9"…$150.00 – 200.00
10"…$200.00 – 250.00

Pitkins & Brooks
FLEUR DE LIS
Salad Bowl
P & B Grade
8"…$125.00 – 150.00

Pitkins & Brooks
SUNBURST FANCY
BOWL
P & B Grade
8"…$125.00 – 150.00

Pitkins & Brooks
EMPRESS SALAD
BOWL
8"…$125.00 – 150.00
9"…$150.00 – 175.00

Pitkins & Brooks
ORIOLE SALAD BOWL
P & B Grade
8"…$80.00 – 95.00

BUTTER TUBS – TRAYS – BUTTERETTES

Averbeck
RUBY
Butter Tub and Plate
Two pieces…$175.00 – 200.00

T. B. Clark & Co.
MANHATTAN
Butter Tub & Plate
Two pieces…$175.00 – 200.00

Averbeck
NAPOLEON
Butter Tub & Plate
Two pieces…$175.00 – 200.00

Averbeck
BOSTON
Butter Tub & Plate
Two pieces…$175.00 – 200.0

J. D. Bergen
SEASIDE
Butter Tub & Plate
Two pieces…$200.00 – 225.00

J. D. Bergen
ELECTRIC
Covered Butter & Plate
Two pieces…$200.00 – 250.00

J. D. Bergen
ORLAND
Covered Butter & Plate
Two pieces…$200.00 – 250.00

Higgins & Seiter
ELITE
Glass Dish
Each…$30.00 – 40.00

J. D. Bergen
PRISM
5"…$50.00 – 60.00
6"…$60.00 – 70.00

Averbeck
SARATOGA
Butterette
Each…$15.00 – 20.00

Averbeck
ASHLAND
Butter Plate
Each…$15.00 – 20.00

J. D. Bergen
RUBY
Handled Butter Plate
5"…$50.00 – 60.00

Averbeck
PRISCILLA
Butterette
3½"…$18.00 – 20.00

Averbeck
LADY CURZON
Butterette
3½"…$18.00 – 20.00

Averbeck
CANTON
Butterette
3½"…$18.00 – 20.00

Averbeck
SPRUCE
Butterette
3½"…$18.00 – 20.00

CANDLESTICKS

J. D. Bergen
3 LIGHT
CANDELABRA
Each ...$200.00 – 250.00

J. D. Bergen
ALBERT
10" Candlestick
Each...$100.00 – 175.00

J. D. Bergen
VICTORIA
Candlestick
7"...$100.00 – 125.00
10"...$150.00 – 175.00

CANDLESTICKS

Pitkins & Brooks
IMPORTED
CANDLESTICK
7½"...$20.00 – 25.00
9¼"...$40.00 – 50.00

Pitkins & Brooks
IMPORTED
CANDLESTICK
7½"...$25.00 – 30.00
9¼"...$40.00 – 50.00
10½"...$60.00 – 75.00

J. D. BERGEN
5 LIGHT
CANDELABRA
Each...$300.00 – 350.00

Pitkins & Brooks
ORO CANDLESTICK
P & B Grade
8"...$125.00 – 150.00

Pitkins & Brooks
HALLE VASE
P & B Grade
12"...$75.00 – 100.00
14"...$100.00 – 125.00
16"...$125.00 – 150.00
18"...$150.00 – 200.00

CARAFES

J. D. Bergen
GOLDENROD
Quart Carafe
Each…$200.00 – 225.00

J. D. Bergen
ARLINGTON
Quart Carafe
Each…$100.00 – 125.00

J. D. Bergen
PROGRESS
Quart Carafe
Each…$150.00 – 200.00

Averbeck
NAPOLEON
Quart …$75.00 – 100.00

Higgins & Seiter
TORNADO
Each…$75.00 – 100.00

Higgins & Seiter
WEBSTER
Quart…$75.00 – 100.00

Higgins & Seiter
MONARCH
Quart…$100.00 – 125.00

J. D. Bergen
NEWPORT
Quart …$75.00 – 100.00

Higgins & Seiter part…

J. D. Bergen
GILMORE
Quart …$100.00 – 125.00

J. D. Bergen
METEOR
Quart …$100.00 – 125.00

27

CARAFES

J. D. Bergen
GOLF
Quart …$100.00 – 125.00

Pitkins & Brooks
WINFIELD CARAFE
Standard Grade
Globe…$75.00 – 100.00

J. D. Bergen
WAVERLY
Quart …$125.00 – 150.00

Averbeck
ACME
Quart …$150.00 – 175.00

J. D. Bergen
U. S.
Quart …$75.00 – 100.00

Averbeck
PRISM
Quart …$100.00 – 125.00

J. D. Bergen
ANSONIA
Quart …$150.00 – 175.00

Pitkins & Brooks
MYRTLE CARAFE
Standard Grade
Globe…$100.00 – 125.00

J. D. Bergen
GOLDENROD
Quart …$150.00 – 175.00

CARAFES

J. D. Bergen
COLONY
Quart…$200.00 – 225.00

J. D. Bergen
MARIE
Quart…$200.00 – 225.00

J. D. Bergen
NEWPORT
Quart…$100.00 – 125.00

T. B. Clark & Co.
MANHATTAN
Quart…$100.00 – 125.00

T. B. Clark & Co.
MANHATTAN
Priscilla Carafe
Quart…$200.00 – 250.00

T. B. Clark & Co.
WINOLA
Quart…$100.00 – 125.00

T. B. Clark
JEWEL
Quart…$100.00 – 125.00

J. D. Bergen
ROLAND
Quart…$100.00 – 125.00

J. D. Bergen
BEDFORD
Quart…$150.00 – 175.00

J. D. Bergen
BALTIMORE
Quart…$150.00 – 175.00

CARAFES

J. D. Bergen
ANSONIA
Quart…$75.00 – 100.00

J. D. Bergen
BEDFORD
Quart…$100.00 – 125.00

J. D. Bergen
WAVERLY
Quart…$150.00 – 175.00

Higgins & Seiter
DIAMOND FAN
Quart …$75.00 – 100.00

T. B. Clark & Co.
WINOLA
Quart…$100.00 – 125.00

Higgins & Seiter
KENMORE
Quart …$75.00 – 100.00

T. B. Clark & Co.
HENRY VIII
Quart…$75.00 – 100.00

J. D. Bergen
ATLAS
Quart…$75.00 – 100.00

J. D. Bergen
U. S.
Quart…$75.00 – 100.00

J. D. Bergen
ORIENT
Quart…$75.00 – 100.00

CARAFES

Pitkins & Brooks
RAJAH GLOBE
P & B Grade
Each…$150.00 – 175.00

Pitkins & Brooks
VENICE CARAFE
Standard Grade
Each…$75.00 – 100.00

Pitkins & Brooks
MARS CARAFE
P & B Grade
Quart…$100.00 – 125.00

Pitkins & Brooks
HEART GLOBE
P & B Grade
Each…$175.00 – 200.00

Averbeck
LIBERTY
Quart …$150.00 – 175.00

Pitkins & Brooks
MEADVILLE CARAFE
Standard Grade
Each…$75.00 – 100.00

T. B. Clark & Co.
MANHATTAN
Quart…$100.00 – 125.00

Averbeck
DAISY
Quart …$125.00 – 150.00

Pitkins & Brooks
SUNBURST
P & B Grade
Each…$100.00 – 125.00

Pitkins & Brooks
CAROLYN GLOBE
P & B Grade
Each…$100.00 – 125.00

Pitkins & Brooks
BELMONT GLOBE
P & B Grade
Each…$100.00 – 125.00

Pitkins & Brooks
CRETE
P & B Grade
Each…$125.00 – 150.00

CARAFES

Pitkins & Brooks
MEADVILLE
Standard Grade
Each...$50.00 – 75.00

Averbeck
GEORGIA
Quart...$75.00 – 100.00

Averbeck
BOSTON
Quart...$125.00 – 150.00

Averbeck
FLORIDA
Quart...$125.00 – 150.00

Averbeck
LADY CURZON
Quart...$75.00 – 100.00

Pitkins & Brooks
IMPORTED
Each...$75.00 – 100.00

Averbeck
RADIUM
Quart...$75.00 – 100.00

Averbeck
VIENNA
Quart...$100.00 – 125.00

Averbeck
TRIXY
Quart...$100.00 – 125.00

Averbeck
MAUD ADAMS
Quart...$100.00 – 125.00

Averbeck
MELBA
Quart...$75.00 – 100.00

CELERY DIPS, SALT DIPS, KNIFE RESTS

Pitkins & Brooks
CELERY DIP
2"...$10.00 – 12.00

Pitkins & Brooks
CELERY DIP
1½"...$10.00 – 12.00

Pitkins & Brooks
CELERY DIP
1⅝"...$15.00 – 18.00

Pitkins & Brooks
CELERY DIP
2"...$5.00 – 8.00

Pitkins & Brooks
CELERY DIP
1¾"...$10.00 – 12.00

Pitkins & Brooks
CELERY DIP
1⅞"...$5.00 – 8.00

Pitkins & Brooks
CELERY DIP
1½"...$5.00 – 8.00

Pitkins & Brooks
CELERY DIP, OVAL
1⅞"...$5.00 – 8.00

Pitkins & Brooks
TABLE SALT
2½"...$5.00 – 8.00

Pitkins & Brooks
AMELIA
Table Salt
3⅛"...$5.00 – 8.00

T. B. Clark & Co.
VENUS
Nest Table Salt
Each...$12.00 – 15.00

J. D. Bergen
DeSOTO
Each...$12.00 – 15.00

J. D. Bergen
SUPERIOR
Each...$10.00 – 12.00

J. D. Bergen
Round Salt
2" Ea. ...$8.00 – 10.00
2¼" Ea. ...$8.00 – 10.00
2½" Ea. ...$12.00 – 15.00
2¾" Ea. ...$12.00 – 15.00

Pitkins & Brooks
KNIFE REST
3½"...$12.00 – 15.00
4½"...$15.00 – 18.00
6"...$18.00 – 20.00

Pitkins & Brooks
KNIFE REST
3½"...$18.00 – 20.00
4½"...$22.00 – 25.00
5½"...$25.00 – 30.00

Pitkins & Brooks
KNIFE REST
3½"...$18.00 – 20.00
4½"...$22.00 – 25.00
5"...$25.00 – 30.00

J. D. Bergen
KNIFE REST
Ind., pair...$15.00 – 18.00
Med., pair...$20.00 – 25.00
Lg., pair...$30.00 – 35.00

Pitkins & Brooks
HEXAGON KNIFE
REST
Standard Grade
4"...$12.00 – 15.00

J. D. Bergen
KNIFE REST
2½", pair...$18.00 – 20.00
3¼", pair...$22.00 – 25.00
5", pair...$25.00 – 30.00

CELERY TRAYS

T. B. Clark & Co.
DORRANCE
Each…$40.00 – 50.00

Higgins & Seiter
WEBSTER
11½"…$75.00 – 100.00

T. B. Clark & Co.
WINOLA
Each…$75.00 – 100.00

Higgins & Seiter
AETNA
4½" x 12"…$60.00 – 75.00

Higgins & Seiter
DELHI
4½" x 11¾"…$60.00 – 75.00

T. B. Clark & Co.
NORDICA
Each…$60.00 – 75.00

J. D. Bergen
STANLEY
6" x 12"…$100.00 – 125.00

J. D. Bergen
MADISON
4½" x 11¾"…$75.00 – 100.00

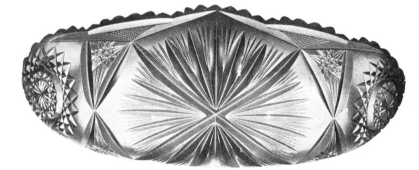

J. D. Bergen
DIADEM
5" x 11"…$75.00 – 100.00

J. D. Bergen
GOLDENROD
5" x 11"…$75.00 – 100.00

CELERY TRAYS

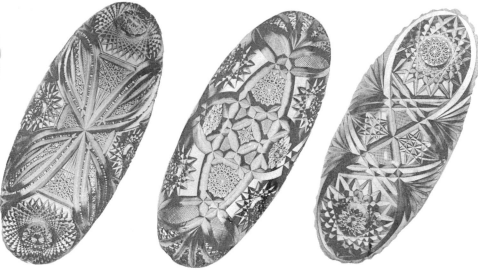

Averbeck
FLEUR DE LIS
11¼"...$75.00 – 100.00

Averbeck
DIAMOND
12"...$100.00 – 125.00

Averbeck
LIBERTY
11¼"...$100.00 – 125.00

Averbeck
RUBY
11¼"...$75.00 – 100.00

Averbeck
LIBERTY
12"...$125.00 – 150.00

Averbeck
FRISCO
12"...$125.00 – 150.00

Averbeck
DIAMOND
11¾"...$125.00 – 150.00

Higgins & Seiter
ST. CLOUD
4" x 11½"...$50.00 – 65.00

T. B. Clark & Co.
MANHATTAN
Each...$60.00 – 75.00

CELERY TRAYS

Pitkins & Brooks
HALLE
P & B Grade
11½"…$100.00 – 125.00

Pitkins & Brooks
BOWA
P & B Grade
12"…$85.00 – 100.00

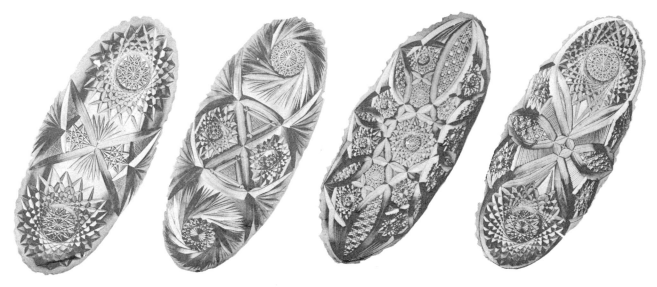

Averbeck
LADY CURZON
11¼"…$100.00 – 125.00

Averbeck
FRISCO
11¼"…$100.00 – 125.00

Averbeck
AMERICAN BEAUTY
11¼"…$100.00 – 125.00

Averbeck
EMPRESS
11¼"…$125.00 – 150.00

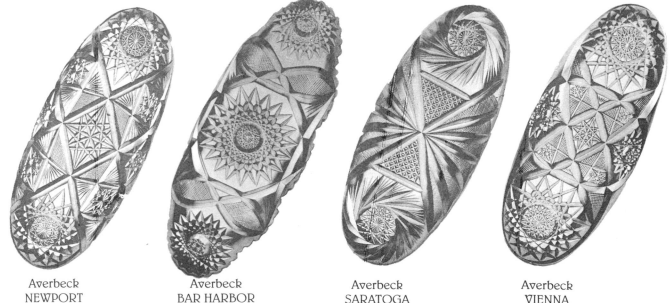

Averbeck
NEWPORT
11¼"…$100.00 – 125.00

Averbeck
BAR HARBOR
11¼"…$100.00 – 125.00

Averbeck
SARATOGA
11¼"…$100.00 – 125.00

Averbeck
VIENNA
11¼"…$125.00 – 150.00

CELERY TRAYS

Pitkins & Brooks
RAJAH
P & B Grade
11¾"...$100.00 – 125.00

Pitkins & Brooks
VENICE
P & B Grade
Each...$100.00 – 125.00

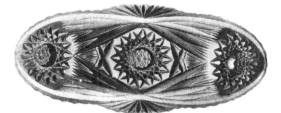

Pitkins & Brooks
MARS
P & B Grade
10¾"...$125.00 – 150.00

Pitkins & Brooks
RAJAH FANCY
P & B Grade
11½"...$150.00 – 200.00

Pitkins & Brooks
MEADVILLE
Standard Grade
11"...$75.00 – 90.00

Pitkins & Brooks
ORIOLE
P & B Grade
Each...$100.00 – 125.00

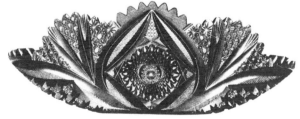

Pitkins & Brooks
ATHOLE
P & B Grade
12"...$100.00 – 125.00

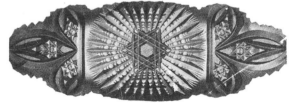

Pitkins & Brooks
EMPRESS
P & B Grade
Each...$150.00 – 200.00

Pitkins & Brooks
PLYMOUTH
P & B Grade
12"...$150.00 – 200.00

Pitkins & Brooks
CORTEZ
P & B Grade
11"...$150.00 – 200.00

CELERY TRAYS

J. D. Bergen
EMBLEM
4½" x 11½"…$125.00 – 150.00

J. D. Bergen
PREMIER
5" x 11"…$100.00 – 125.00

J. D. Bergen
OTHELLO
4½" x 11¾"…$100.00 – 125.00

J. D. Bergen
ADELPHI
6" x 13"…$175.00 – 200.00

J. D. Bergen
GROVE
6" x 13"…$175.00 – 200.00

T. B. Clark & Co.
DESDEMONA
Each…$60.00 – 75.00

Higgins & Seiter
ARLINGTON
11½" x 4¼"…$60.00 – 75.00

T. B. Clark & Co.
ADONIS
Each…$60.00 – 75.00

Higgins & Seiter
5½" x 12"…$60.00 – 75.00

CELERY TRAYS

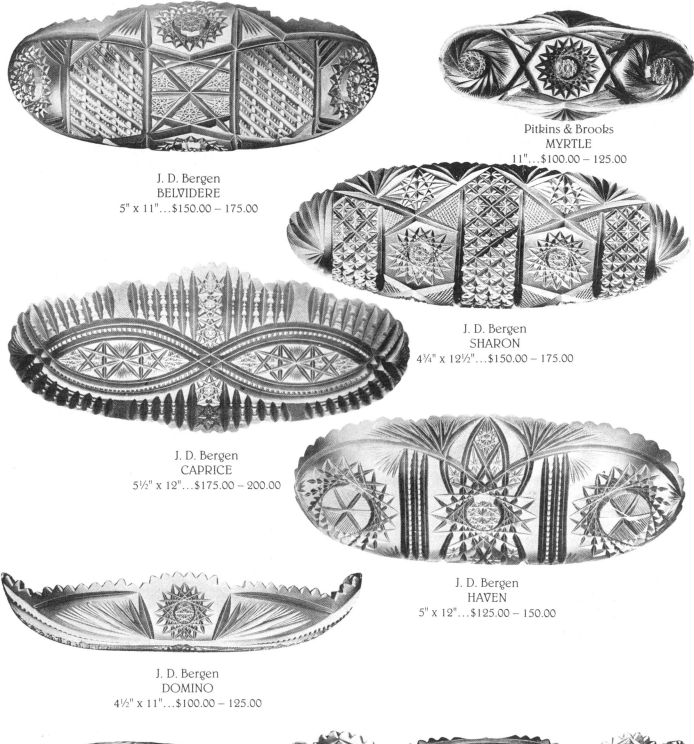

J. D. Bergen
BELVIDERE
5" x 11"...$150.00 – 175.00

Pitkins & Brooks
MYRTLE
11"...$100.00 – 125.00

J. D. Bergen
SHARON
4¾" x 12½"...$150.00 – 175.00

J. D. Bergen
CAPRICE
5½" x 12"...$175.00 – 200.00

J. D. Bergen
HAVEN
5" x 12"...$125.00 – 150.00

J. D. Bergen
DOMINO
4½" x 11"...$100.00 – 125.00

Pitkins & Brooks
NELLORE
P & B Grade
Each...$100.00 – 125.00

J. D. Bergen
EMERSON
6" x 12"...$150.00 – 200.00

CHEESE PLATES AND MAYONNAISE

Higgins & Seiter
WEBSTER
Complete…$250.00 – 300.00

T. B. Clark & Co.
MANHATTAN
Cheese Cover & Plate
Complete…$250.00 – 300.00

Higins & Seiter
NEW YORK
9"…$250.00 – 300.00
10"…$300.00 – 350.00

J. D. Bergen
GLENWOOD
5"…$150.00 – 175.00
6"…$175.00 – 200.00

J. D. Bergen
IRENE
Whipped Cream Bowl
3 Handled
6"…$75.00 – 100.00

Averbeck
GEORGIA
Mayonnaise Set
Bowl & Plate
Set…$75.00 – 100.00

Higgins & Seiter
NAPOLEON
Bowl & Plate
Set…$125.00 – 150.00

J. D. Bergen
BURLINGTON
Whipped Cream Bowl
6"…$100.00 – 125.00

Averbeck
RADIUM
Mayonnaise Set
Bowl & Plate
5"…$75.00 – 100.00

Averbeck
LIBERTY
Mayonnaise Bowl
Each…$75.00 – 100.00

Higgins & Seiter
FLORENTINE
Mayonnaise Set
Bowl & Plate
Set…$125.00 – 150.00

Higgins & Seiter
IMPERIAL
Mayonnaise Set
Bowl & Tray
Set…$125.00 – 150.00

CIGAR JARS

Pitkins & Brooks
ZESTA CIGAR JAR
P & B Grade
8½"…$200.00 – 250.00

Higgins & Seiter
Cigar Jar
Top made hollow for
holding sponge.
50 white…$150.00 – 200.00
25 white…$125.00 – 150.00
50 green…$200.00 – 250.00
25 green…$150.00 – 200.00

Higgins & Seiter
CIGAR JAR
With feame in either
mahogany or antique oak.
50 Cigars…$175.00 – 200.00

Higgins & Seiter
MAJESTIC
6½"…$150.00 – 200.00

Higgins & Seiter
Cigar Jar
Top made hollow for
holding sponge.
50 white…$150.00 – 200.00
25 white…$125.00 – 150.00
50 green…$200.00 – 250.00
25 green…$150.00 – 200.00

J. D. Bergen
GLENWOOD
50 cigars …$200.00 – 250.00
Cigarette…$150.00 – 200.00

Higgins & Seiter
Top made hollow for
holding sponge.
50 white…$150.00 – 200.00
25 white…$125.00 – 150.00
50 green…$200.00 – 250.00
25 green…$150.00 – 200.00

J. D. Bergen
SEASIDE
25 Cigars …$200.00 – 225.00

TOBACCO JARS & COLOGNE BOTTLES

J. D. Bergen
WAGNER
7" Cologne…$75.00 – 85.00
7½" Cologne…$85.00 – 100.00
8½" Cologne…$100.00 – 125.00

J. D. Bergen
PREMIER
Tobacco Jar
7½"…$200.00 – 250.00

J. D. Bergen
MEDORA
7" Cologne…$75.00 – 85.00
7½" Cologne…$85.00 – 100.00
8½" Cologne…$100.00 – 125.00

J. D. Bergen
PRISM
7" Cologne…$60.00 – 65.00
8" Cologne…$65.00 – 70.00
9" Cologne…$75.00 – 100.00

Pitkins & Brooks
IMPORTED COLOGNE
3 oz.…$30.00 – 35.00
7 oz.…$45.00 – 55.00
9 oz.…$75.00 – 100.00

Pitkins & Brooks
ENO COLOGNE
P & B Grade
4 oz.…$50.00 – 60.00
6 oz.…$60.00 – 75.00
8 oz.…$75.00 – 90.00

J. D. Bergen
PREMIER
5" Cologne…$55.00 – 60.00
6" Cologne…$65.00 – 75.00
7" Cologne…$75.00 – 85.00
8" Cologne…$85.00 – 100.00

Averbeck
RADIUM
3½" Cologne…$40.00 – 50.00
4½" Cologne…$50.00 – 65.00
5½" Cologne…$75.00 – 90.00

Pitkins & Brooks
SUNBURST COLOGNE
P & B Grade
6 oz.…$65.00 – 75.00
8 oz.…$75.00 – 100.00

Pitkins & Brooks
CAROLYN COLOGNE
P & B Grade
6 oz.…$65.00 – 75.00

Pitkins & Brooks
IMPORTED COLOGNE
3 oz.…$40.00 – 50.00
5 oz.…$60.00 – 75.00

Pitkins & Brooks
IMPORTED COLOGI
3 oz.…$30.00 – 40.0
5 oz.…$40.00 – 50.0
8 oz.…$60.00 – 75.0

COLOGNE BOTTLES

Pitkins & Brooks
BERRIE COLOGNE
P & B Grade
5 oz....$50.00 – 60.00
8 oz....$60.00 – 75.00

Pitkins & Brooks
BERRIE COLOGNE
P & B Grade
5 oz....$75.00 – 85.00

Pitkins & Brooks
AURORA BOREALIS
COLOGNE
P & B Grade
6 oz....$80.00 – 90.00

Pitkins & Brooks
ELECTRA TOILET
WATER BOTTLE
P & B Grade
8 oz....$85.00 – 100.00

Pitkins & Brooks
KING GEORGE
COLOGNE
P & B Grade
8 oz....$85.00 – 100.00

Pitkins & Brooks
BERMUDA COLOGNE
P & B Grade
6 oz....$100.00 – 125.00

Pitkins & Brooks
PRISM RUM BOTTLE
P & B Grade
9½" oz....$65.00 – 75.00

Pitkins & Brooks
MARS COLOGNE
P & B Grade
6 oz....$65.00 – 75.00
8 oz....$85.00 – 100.00

Pitkins & Brooks
HALLE COLOGNE
P & B Grade
6 oz....$65.00 – 75.00
10 oz....$100.00 – 125.00

Pitkins & Brooks
BELMONT COLOGNE
P & B Grade
6 oz....$65.00 – 75.00
10 oz....$100.00 – 125.00

T. B. Clark & Co.
SQUARE COLOGNE,
ST. GEORGE
8 oz....$75.00 – 95.00
12 oz....$100.00 – 125.00

T. B. Clark & Co.
ROUND COLOGNE,
JEWEL
6 oz....$40.00 – 50.00
8 oz....$55.00 – 65.00
12 oz....$75.00 – 100.00

T. B. Clark & Co.
GLOBE COLOGNE,
JEWEL
24 oz....$100.00 – 125.00
18 oz....$75.00 – 100.00
9 oz....$50.00 – 65.00
6 oz....$40.00 – 50.00

Higgins & Seiter
ST. JULIEN
4 oz....$40.00 – 50.00
6 oz....$50.00 – 60.00
8 oz....$65.00 – 75.00
12 oz....$75.00 – 85.00

COMB AND BRUSH TRAYS, PIN HOLDERS, POMADE JARS

Pitkins & Brooks
ELECTRA COMB &
BRUSH TRAY
P & B Grade
11"…$300.00 – 350.00

Pitkins & Brooks
ALADDIN COMB &
BRUSH TRAY
P & B Grade
12"…$300.00 – 350.00

Pitkins & Brooks
DELMAR COMB &
BRUSH TRAY
P & B Grade
11"…$200.00 – 250.00

Pitkins & Brooks
ELECTRA POMADE
BOX
P & B Grade
2¾"…$100.00 – 125.00

J. D. Bergen
PRISM
Pomade Jar
Each…$75.00 – 90.00

Pitkins & Brooks
ELECTRA HAT PIN
HOLDER
P & B Grade
7"…$175.00 – 225.00

Averbeck
RUBY
Pin or Olive Tray
Each…$40.00 – 50.00

J. D. Bergen
SPLIT & HOLLOW
Pin Tray
Each…$40.00 – 50.00

COMPORTS

J. D. Bergen
BERMUDA
High-footed Comport
8"...$100.00 – 125.00

Pitkins & Brooks
EMPIRE FOOTED
BOWL
P & B Grade
(2 pieces)
Set...$250.00 – 300.00

Averbeck
VIENNA
Each...$200.00 – 250.00

Pitkins & Brooks
MEMPHIS
5" (dia)...$100.00 – 125.00
6" (dia)...$125.00 – 150.00
7" (dia)...$150.00 – 175.00

Pitkins & Brooks
HEART
P & B Grade
9" x 5"...$175.00 – 200.00

Pitkins & Brooks
CRETE
P & B Grade
5"...$100.00 – 125.00

Averbeck
RADIUM
Bonbon with Foot
6"...$100.00 – 125.00

Pitkins & Brooks
MARS FOOTED
FRUIT BOWL
P & B Grade
8"...$150.00 – 200.00

Averbeck
LONDON
Spoon Dish with Foot
7½"...$150.00 – 200.00

COMPORTS

Pitkins & Brooks
HURON
P & B Grade
Each...$100.00 – 125.00

Pitkins & Brooks
HEART
P & B Grade
7½"...$125.00 – 150.00

Pitkins & Brooks
SAVANNAH COMPORT
ENGRAVED
P & B Grade
7"...$125.00 – 150.00

Pitkins & Brooks
AUTO COMPORT
P & B Grade
Each...$175.00 – 200.00

Pitkins & Brooks
HALLE COMPORT
P & B Grade
5"...$125.00 – 150.00

Pitkins & Brooks
MYRTLE COMPORT
Standard Grade
5"...$100.00 – 125.00
7"...$150.00 – 200.00

Pitkins & Brooks
McKINLEY COMPORT
P & B Grade
7"...$175.00 – 200.00

Pitkins & Brooks
TOPAZ COMPORT
P & B Grade
9" x 6"...$175.00 – 200.00

Pitkins & Brooks
GLEE COMPORT
P & B Grade
8" x 7½"...$250.00 – 300.00

COMPORTS

Averbeck
NAPLES
9½"…$100.00 – 125.00

Averbeck
GEORGIA
Each…$250.00 – 300.00

Averbeck
DIAMOND
Each…$250.00 – 300.00

Averbeck
NICE
10¼"…$150.00 – 175.00

Pitkins & Brooks
ATLAS
12" x 6"…$150.00 – 175.00

Pitkins & Brooks
HALLE COMPORT
P & B Grade
Each…$100.00 – 125.00

Pitkins & Brooks
RAJAH
P & B Grade
8"…$140.00 – 160.00
10"…$175.00 – 200.00
12"…$200.00 – 225.00
14"…$250.00 – 300.00

Pitkins & Brooks
ALEXIS
P & B Grade
Each…$100.00 – 125.00

Averbeck
MAUD ADAMS
Each…$150.00 – 175.00

Pitkins & Brooks
VILLA
P & B Grade
5"…$75.00 – 100.00

COMPORTS

Pitkins & Brooks
ZELLER
P & B Grade
7" x 5"…$60.00 – 75.00

J. D. Bergen
MAGNET
5"…$60.00 – 75.00
6"…$85.00 – 100.00

Pitkins & Brooks
ATLAS
P & B Grade
9" x 6"…$150.00 – 200.00

J. D. Bergen
BEACON
6"…$125.00 – 150.00

J. D. Bergen
ENTERPRISE
6"…$75.00 – 90.00
7"…$100.00 – 125.00
8"…$125.00 – 150.00
9"…$150.00 – 175.00
10"…$200.00 – 250.00

Averbeck
LIBERTY
Each…$150.00 – 175.00

J. D. Bergen
WALTHAM
6"…$150.00 – 175.00

Pitkins & Brooks
BORDER
(2 Handle)
P & B Grade
10"…$175.00 – 200.00

Averbeck
LONDON
Each…$250.00 – 300.00

Pitkins & Brooks
CRESS
P & B Grade
5"…$50.00 – 65.00
6"…$75.00 – 85.00

Pitkins & Brooks
SEPIA
P & B Grade
Each…$100.00 – 125.00

Averbeck
TRIXY
Each…$150.00 – 175.00

Pitkins & Brooks
IMPORTED COMPORT
5"…$40.00 – 50.00
6"…$50.00 – 60.00
7"…$60.00 – 70.00
8"…$75.00 – 90.00

COMPORTS

J. D. Bergen
MARCUS
7"...$125.00 – 150.00
8"...$150.00 – 175.00
9"...$200.00 – 250.00

T. B. Clark & Co.
MANHATTAN
6"...$90.00 – 100.00

J. D. Bergen
CARMEN
High Foot Comport
Each...$125.00 – 150.00
Each...$150.00 – 175.00
Each...$175.00 – 200.00
(Original catalog did
not have sizes listed.)

J. D. Bergen
WATSON
6"...$100.00 – 150.00
7"...$150.00 – 200.00
8"...$200.00 – 250.00
9"...$250.00 – 300.00

J. D. Bergen
ARCADIA
Each...$300.00 – 350.00

CORDIAL SETS AND WHISKEY SETS

J. D. Bergen
SAVOY
Set...$1,250.00 – 1,500.00

J. D. Bergen
GLENWOOD
Set...$450.00 – 550.00

J. D. Bergen
PREMIER
Set...$500.00 – 550.00

CORDIAL SETS AND WHISKEY SETS

J. D. Bergen
GLENWOOD
Set…$400.00 – 450.00

J. D. Bergen
GLENWOOD
Set…$500.00 – 550.00

J. D. Bergen
ELECTRIC
Set…$300.00 – 400.00

J. D. Bergen
ELECTRIC
Set…$500.00 – 550.00

CORDIAL SETS AND WHISKEY SETS

Higgins & Seiter
WEBSTER
Set…$600.00 – 750.00

Higgins & Seiter
SYROTT
Set…$400.00 – 450.00

Higgins & Seiter
CONCORD
Set…$400.00 – 450.00

Higgins & Seiter
MANILLA
Set…$400.00 – 450.00

Higgins & Seiter
COLONIAL
Set…$100.00 – 150.00

Higgins & Seiter
HENRIETTA
Set…$350.00 – 450.00

CORDIAL SETS AND WHISKEY SETS

Higgins & Selter
GEORGIA
2 bottles ...$400.00 – 450.00
3 bottles ...$600.00 – 675.00

Higgins & Seiter
DEWEY
2 bottles ...$250.00 – 300.00

CREAM AND SUGAR

J. D. Bergen
GLENWOOD
Cream…$35.00 – 40.00

J. D. Bergen
GLENWOOD
Sugar…$50.00 – 65.00

J. D. Bergen
DETROIT
Half Pint Footed
Cream…$50.00 – 65.00

J. D. Bergen
OREGON
Half Pint
Cream…$35.00 – 45.00

J. D. Bergen
DETROIT
Footed
Sugar…$50.00 – 65.00

J. D. Bergen
GOLF
Sugar…$30.00 – 35.00

J. D. Bergen
GILBERT
Sugar…$35.00 – 40.00

J. D. Bergen
SUPERIOR
Half Pint
Cream…$45.00 – 55.00

J. D. Bergen
MAGNET
Sugar…$25.00 – 30.00

Higgins & Seiter
ARLINGTON
Sugar & Creamer
Set….$50.00 – 60.00

Higgins & Seiter
WASHINGTON
Sugar & Creamer
Set….$50.00 – 65.00

Higgins & Seiter
WEBSTER
Sugar & Creamer
Set….$70.00 – 85.00

Higgins & Seiter
BE VEDERE
Sugar & Creamer
Set….$50.00 – 65.00

CREAM AND SUGAR

J. D. Bergen
GOLF
Half Pint Cream
Each…$30.00 – 35.00

J. D. Bergen
AVON
Sugar…$30.00 – 35.00

J. D. Bergen
EMBLEM
Sugar…$35.00 – 40.00

J. D. Bergen
AVON
Cream…$30.00 – 35.00

J. D. Bergen
GILBERT
Half Pint Cream
Each…$40.00 – 50.00

J. D. Bergen
GOLF
Half Pint Cream
Each…$30.00 – 35.00

J. D. Bergen
EMBLEM
Half Pint Cream
Each…$35.00 – 40.00

J. D. Bergen
MAGNET
Half Pint Cream
Each…$25.00 – 30.00

J. D. Bergen
GRACE
Half Pint Cream
Each…$40.00 – 50.00

J. D. Bergen
GRACE
Sugar…$40.00 – 50.00

J. D. Bergen
GOLF
Sugar…$30.00 – 35.00

J. D. Bergen
SUPERIOR
Sugar…$45.00 – 55.00

J. D. Bergen
OREGON
Sugar…$35.00 – 45.00

J. D. Bergen
BEDFORD
Half Pint Cream
Each…$35.00 – 45.00

J. D. Bergen
BEDFORD
Sugar…$35.00 – 45.00

CREAM AND SUGAR

Averbeck
MELBA
Cream & Sugar
Set…$85.00 – 100.00

Averbeck
GEORGIA
Cream & Sugar
Set…$85.00 – 100.00

Averbeck
SARATOGA
Cream & Sugar
Set…$85.00 – 100.00

Averbeck
LIBERTY
Cream & Sugar
Set…$85.00 – 100.00

Averbeck
VIENNA
Cream & Sugar
Set…$85.00 – 100.00

Averbeck
FLORIDA
Cream & Sugar
Each…$65.00 – 80.00

Averbeck
LADY CURZON
Cream & Sugar
Set…$85.00 – 100.00

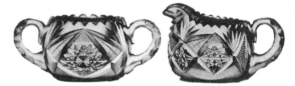

Averbeck
RUBY
Cream & Sugar
Set…$85.00 – 100.00

Averbeck
LIBERTY
Cream & Sugar
Set…$100.00 – 125.00

Averbeck
AMERICAN BEAUTY
Cream & Sugar
Set…$150.00 – 175.00

Averbeck
PRISCILLA
Cream & Sugar
Set…$65.00 – 80.00

Averbeck
RUBY
Half Pint Cream
Each…$75.00 – 85.00

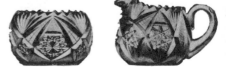

Averbeck
FLORIDA
Cream & Sugar
Set…$65.00 – 80.00

CREAM AND SUGAR

Pitkins & Brooks
BORDER
Sugar & Cream
P & B Grade
Set…$75.00 – 100.00

Pitkins & Brooks
SUNBURST
Sugar & Cream
P & B Grade
Set…$125.00 – 150.00

Pitkins & Brooks
CAROLYN
P & B Grade
Set…$125.00 – 150.00

Pitkins & Brooks
RAJAH
P & B Grade
Set…$150.00 – 175.00

Pitkins & Brooks
TRIUMPH
P & B Grade
Set…$85.00 – 100.00

Pitkins & Brooks
MEADVILLE
Standard Grade
Set…$60.00 – 75.00

Pitkins & Brooks
PLYMOUTH
P & B Grade
Set…$150.00 – 175.00

Pitkins & Brooks
DUCHESS
P & B Grade
Set…$150.00 – 175.00

Pitkins & Brooks
GARLAND
P & B Grade
Set…$150.00 – 175.00

Pitkins & Brooks
PRISM
P & B Grade
Set…$85.00 – 100.00

CREAM AND SUGAR

Pitkins & Brooks
ORIOLE
P & B Grade
Set…$85.00 – 100.00

Pitkins & Brooks
MYRTLE
Standard Grade
Set…$85.00 – 100.00

Pitkins & Brooks
BYRNS
P & B Grade
Set…$125.00 – 150.00

Pitkins & Brooks
MARS
P & B Grade
Set…$125.00 – 150.00

Pitkins & Brooks
HALLE
P & B Grade
Set…$150.00 – 175.00

Pitkins & Brooks
VENICE
P & B Grade
Set…$100.00 – 125.00

Pitkins & Brooks
BELMONT
P & B Grade
Set…$100.00 – 125.00

Pitkins & Brooks
NORTHERN STAR
P & B Grade
Set…$175.00 – 200.00

Pitkins & Brooks
ORIOLE
P & B Grade
Set…$65.00 – 75.00

Pitkins & Brooks
HEART
P & B Grade
Set…$175.00 – 200.00

CREAM AND SUGAR

T. B. Clark & Co.
VENUS
Set…$200.00 – 225.00

T. B. Clark & Co.
WINOLA
Lg. Set…$85.00 – 100.00
Sm. Set….$65.00 – 80.00

Higgins & Seiter
ARLINGTON
Set…$65.00 – 80.00

T. B. Clark & Co.
ARBUTUS
Set…$80.00 – 100.00

CUPS

Averbeck
VIENNA
Cup…$18.00 – 20.00

J. D. Bergen
ELECTRIC
Cup…$18.00 – 20.00

J. D. Bergen
GOLF
Cup…$18.00 – 20.00

J. D. Bergen
WABASH
Cup…$18.00 – 20.00

J. D. Bergen
KENWOOD
Cup…$30.00 – 35.00

J. D. Bergen
PREMIER
Cup…$18.00 – 20.00

T. B. Clark & Co.
Punch Cup & Plate
Set…$45.00 – 55.00

T. B. Clark & Co.
WINOLA
Cup…$18.00 – 20.00

T. B. Clark & Co.
Handled Lemonade
Cup…$20.00 – 22.00

CRUETS AND OIL BOTTLES

J. D. Bergen
OREGON
Half Pint Oil
Each…$60.00 – 75.00

J. D. Bergen
GOLF
Half Pint Oil
Each…$75.00 – 90.00

J. D. Bergen
WAVERLY
Half Pint Oil
Each…$100.00 – 125.00

J. D. Bergen
WAVERLY
Half Pint Oil
Each…$100.00 – 125.00

J. D. Bergen
GARLAND
Half Pint Cruet
Each…$125.00 – 150.00

J. D. Bergen
WAVERLY
Third pt. …$100.00 – 125.00
Half pt. …$100.00 – 125.00

Pitkins & Brooks
GARLAND OIL
Each…$50.00 – 60.00

Pitkins & Brooks
IMPORTED OIL
Each…$20.00 – 22.00

Pitkins & Brooks
IMPORTED OIL
Each…$15.00 – 18.00

J. D. Bergen
VIOLA
Half Pint Cruet
Each…$125.00 – 150.00

J. D. Bergen
PRISM
Half Pint Oil
Each…$60.00 – 75.00

J. D. Bergen
PALACE
Half Pint Oil
Each…$75.00 – 90.00

CRUETS AND OIL BOTTLES

Pitkins & Brooks
IMPORTED OIL
Each…$35.00 – 45.00

Averbeck
FLORIDA
7½"…$75.00 – 85.00

Pitkins & Brooks
IMPORTED OIL
6"…$65.00 – 75.00

Pitkins & Brooks
MIKADO SQUAT OIL
P & B Grade
6"…$65.00 – 75.00

Higgins & Seiter
PRISM
5"…$35.00 – 45.00

Higgins & Seiter
NAPOLEON
Half Pint…$75.00 – 90.00

Higgins & Seiter
STRAWBERRY
DIAMOND & FAN
½" Pint…$75.00 – 90.00

Pitkins & Brooks
IMPORTED OIL
6"…$20.00 – 22.00

Higgins & Seiter
NAPOLEON
Each…$100.00 – 125.00

Higgins & Seiter
WEBSTER
Each…$60.00 – 75.00

T. B. Clark & Co.
MANHATTAN
Each…$60.00 – 75.00

T. B. Clark & Co.
HURON
Each…$60.00 – 75.00

Pitkins & Brooks
STANDARD OIL
7"…$22.00 – 25.00

Pitkins & Brooks
IMPORTED OIL
6"…$18.00 – 20.00

Pitkins & Brooks
IMPORTED OIL
6"…$30.00 – 35.00

Pitkins & Brooks
BALTIC SQUAT OIL
Standard Grade
Plain handle…$40.00 – 50.00
Cut handle…$60.00 – 75.00

Pitkins & Brooks
BERMUDA OIL
P & B Grade
8½"…$150.00 – 175.00

CRUETS AND OIL BOTTLES

J. D. Bergen
GOLF
Third Pint Oil
Each…$65.00 – 75.00

Pitkins & Brooks
KING GEORGE OIL
P & B Grade
Each…$65.00 – 75.00

Pitkins & Brooks
RICHELIEU OIL
9¾"…$35.00 – 40.00

Pitkins & Brooks
ALADDIN OIL
P & B Grade
Each…$150.00 – 175.00

J. D. Bergen
ELECTRIC
Half Pint Oil
Each…$100.00 – 110.00

Pitkins & Brooks
SUNRAY GLOBE
Standard Grade
Each…$75.00 – 90.00

Higgins & Seiter
FLORENTINE
Each…$50.00 – 65.00

Higgins & Seiter
CUBA
Half Pint Oil
Each…$45.00 – 55.00

Higgins & Seiter
Each…$50.00 – 65.00

Pitkins & Brooks
IMPORTED OIL
7½"…$25.00 – 35.00

J. D. Bergen
PREMIER
Third Pt. …$65.00 – 75.00
Half Pt. …$85.00 – 100.00

Pitkins & Brooks
SQUAT OIL
6"…$75.00 – 90.00

Pitkins & Brooks
IMPORTED OIL
6"…$25.00 – 35.00

J. D. Bergen
BERKSHIRE
Third Pt. …$65.00 – 75.00
Half Pt. …$85.00 – 100.00

CUPS

| Pitkins & Brooks Standard Grade $10.00 – 12.00 | Pitkins & Brooks Standard Grade $18.00 – 20.00 | Pitkins & Brooks $18.00 – 20.00 | Pitkins & Brooks Standard Grade $20.00 – 22.00 | Pitkins & Brooks P & B Grade $20.00 – 22.00 | Pitkins & Brooks Standard Grade $18.00 – 20.00 |

| Pitkins & Brooks SUNBURST P & B Grade $20.00 – 22.00 | Pitkins & Brooks P & B Grade $30.00 – 35.00 | Pitkins & Brooks $10.00 – 12.00 | Pitkins & Brooks Standard Grade $4.00 – 6.00 | Pitkins & Brooks GARLAND P & B Grade $20.00 – 22.00 | Pitkins & Brooks $10.00 – 12.00 |

| Pitkins & Brooks CAROLYN P & B Grade $20.00 – 22.00 | Pitkins & Brooks MARS P & B Grade $20.00 – 22.00 | Pitkins & Brooks HALLE P & B Grade $30.00 – 35.00 | Pitkins & Brooks BELMONT P & B Grade $20.00 – 22.00 | Pitkins & Brooks RAJAH P & B Grade $30.00 – 35.00 | Pitkins & Brooks P & B Grade $20.00 – 22.00 |

| Pitkins & Brooks ORIOLE P & B Grade $22.00 – 25.00 | Pitkins & Brooks HEART P & B Grade $30.00 – 35.00 | Pitkins & Brooks MEADVILLE Standard Grade $22.00 –25.00 | Pitkins & Brooks RAJAH P & B Grade $35.00 – 40.00 | Averbeck TRIXY $20.00 – 25.00 |

| J. D. Bergen MARLOW $22.00 – 25.00 | J. D. Bergen CONSAIR $22.00 – 25.00 | J. D. Bergen PROGRESS $22.00 – 25.00 | J. D. Bergen EDNA $22.00 – 25.00 |

| J. D. Bergen WABASH $30.00 – 35.00 | Averbeck OCCIDENT $35.00 – 40.00 | J. D. Bergen ELECTRIC $20.00 – 25.00 | J. D. Bergen MONTICELLO $30.00 – 35.00 | J. D. Bergen PREMIER $30.00 – 35.00 |

DECANTERS AND JUGS

J. D. Bergen
GLENWOOD
1 Qt. ...$150.00 – 200.00

J. D. Bergen
ANSONIA
1 Qt. ...$200.00 – 225.00

J. D. Bergen
MARIE
1 Qt. ...$300.00 – 350.00

J. D. Bergen
ELECTRIC
1 Qt. ...$125.00 – 150.00

J. D. Bergen
GOLF
1 Pt. ...$100.00 – 125.00

Averbeck
ACME
9¼"...$200.00 – 250.00

Averbeck
ALABAMA
1 Qt. ...$175.00 – 200.00

DECANTERS AND JUGS

J. D. Bergen
GOLF
1 Pt. ...$100.00 – 125.00
1 Qt. ...$125.00 – 150.00

J. D. Bergen
ELECTRIC
1 Pt. ...$150.00 – 175.00
1 Qt. ...$175.00 – 200.00

J. D. Bergen
ELECTRIC
1 Pt. ...$100.00 – 125.00
1 Qt. ...$125.00 – 150.00

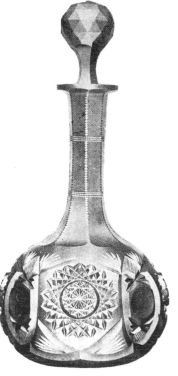

J. D. Bergen
SAVOY
1 Pt. ...$100.00 – 125.00
1 Qt. ...$125.00 – 150.00

J. D. Bergen
GOLF
1 Pt. ...$100.00 – 125.00
1 Qt. ...$125.00 – 150.00

J. D. Bergen
ANSONIA
1 Qt. ...$225.00 – 250.00

DECANTERS AND JUGS

Pitkins & Brooks
GARLAND
1 Qt. ...$125.00 – 150.00

J. D. Bergen
SAVOY
1 Pt. ...$200.00 – 225.00
1 Qt. ...$225.00 – 250.00

J. D. Bergen
ALERT
1 Pt. ...$100.00 – 125.00
1 Qt. ...$125.00 – 150.00

J. D. Bergen
BEAUMONT
1 Pt. ...$200.00 – 225.00

Averbeck
RADIUM
1 Pt. ...$100.00 – 125.00
1 Qt. ...$150.00 – 200.00

J. D. Bergen
CLARION
1 Qt. ...$250.00 – 300.00

Pitkins & Brooks
KING GEORGE
P & B Grade
Each...$100.00 – 125.00

DECANTERS AND JUGS

J. D. Bergen
MARIE
1 Qt. ...$200.00 – 250.00

Pitkins & Brooks
ALADDIN
P & B Grade
Each...$150.00 – 200.00

J. D. Bergen
ASHTON
1 Qt. ...$200.00 – 250.00

J. D. Bergen
SAVOY
3 Pt. ...$175.00 – 200.00

J. D. Bergen
GLENWOOD
1 Qt. ...$195.00 – 200.00

Pitkins & Brooks
DELMAR
P & B Grade
Each...$65.00 – 75.00

Averbeck
GENOA
Each...$200.00 – 250.00

J. D. Bergen
GLENWOOD
1 Qt. ...$150.00 – 200.00

DECANTERS AND JUGS

Higgins & Seiter
GEORGIA
13"...$175.00 – 200.00

Higgins & Seiter
Decanter...$175.00 – 200.00
Claret Jug...$200.00 – 225.00

Higgins & Seiter
ELECTRIC
15"...$200.00 – 225.00

Higgins & Seiter
ELECTRIC
15"...$175.00 – 200.00

Higgins & Seiter
RENAISSANCE
White...$60.00 – 75.00
Green or Ruby...$150.00 – 175.00

T. B. Clark & Co.
WIDE MOUTH JUG
JEWEL
½ Pt. ...$60.00 – 75.00
Pt. ...$75.00 – 90.00
Qt. ...$90.00 – 110.00
3 Pt. ...$110.00 – 125.00
½ Gal. ...$125.00 – 150.00

Higgins & Seiter
YACHT SHAPE
White...$40.00 – 50.00
Green...$55.00 – 60.00
Ruby...$60.00 – 75.00

Pitkins & Brooks
DELMAR
P & B Grade
Each...$150.00 – 175.00

Pitkins & Brooks
ELECTRIC
P & B Grade
Qt. ...$200.00 – 225.00

J. D. Bergen
GOLF
½ Pt. ...$75.00 – 100.00

Higgins & Seiter
NAPOLEON
Pt. ....$100.00 – 125.00
Qt. ...$125.00 – 150.00
Pt. Claret...$150.00 – 175.00
Qt. Claret...$175.00 – 200.00

Higgins & Seiter
FLORENTINE
Clarets...$125.00 – 150.00
Wines...$100.00 – 120.00
Sherries...$100.00 – 120.00

DECANTERS AND JUGS

Averbeck
LIBERTY
9¼"...$200.00 – 250.00

Higgins & Seiter
FLORENTINE
Each...$150.00 – 175.00

Higgins & Seiter
STRAWBERRY
DIAMOND FAN
½ Pt. ...$75.00 – 85.00
Pt. ...$85.00 – 95.00
Qt. ...$100.00 – 110.00
½ Pt. Claret...$75.00 – 85.00
Pt. Claret...$85.00 – 95.00
Qt. Claret ...$100.00 – 110.00
Qt. Water...$100.00 – 110.00

Higgins & Seiter
Clarets...$175.00 – 200.00
Wine...$175.00 – 200.00

T. B. Clark & Co.
HENRY VIII
Qt. Tankard Jug
Each...$150.00 – 195.00

T. B. Clark & Co.
WINOLA
Qt. Jug
Each...$125.00 – 150.00

T. B. Clark & Co.
ADONIS
Flemish Jug
Each...$300.00 – 350.00

T. B. Clark & Co.
VENUS
Wiskey Flagon
Each...$200.00 – 225.00

T. B. Clark & Co.
VENUS
Wide Mouth Jug
Pt. ...$150.00 – 175.00
Qt. ...$175.00 – 200.00
3 Pt. ...$200.00 – 225.00

T. B. Clark & Co.
DESDEMONA
Priscilla Jug
Each...$350.00 – 400.00

Higgins & Seiter
MANILLA
Whiskey Jug
Each ...$175.00 – 200.00

T. B. Clark & Co.
WINOLA
Wide Mouth Jug
½ Pt. ...$60.00 – 75.00
Pt. ...$75.00 – 90.00
Qt. ...$90.00 – 110.00
3 Pt. ...$110.00 – 125.00
½ Gal. ...$125.00 – 150.00

DECANTERS AND JUGS

T. B. Clark & Co.
STRAW & FAN
Qt. with handle…$110.00 – 125.00
Without handle…$100.00 – 110.00

T. B. Clark & CO.
WINOLA
Quart handled
Each…$125.00 – 150.00

J. D. Bergen
SAVOY
3 Pt. ….$250.00 – 300.00

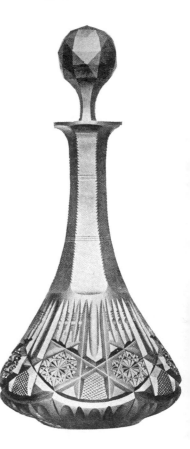

J. D. Bergen
ELECTRIC
Pt. …$125.00 – 150.00

Pitkins & Brooks
DELMAR
P & B GRADE
Each…$125.00 – 150.00

Averbeck
LIBERTY
Each…$200.00 – 225.00

J. D. Bergen
GLENWOOD
1 Qt. …$150.00 – 175.00

DECANTERS AND JUGS

Higgins & Seiter
CLARET JUG
Qt. …$110.00 – 125.00
Qt. Claret…$125.00 – 150.00
Pt. …$100.00 – 110.00
Pt. Claret…$125.00 – 150.00

T. B. Clark & Co.
WINOLA
Qt. No Handle
Each…$125.00 – 150.00

Averbeck
FLORIDA
Pt. …$125.00 – 150.00
Qt. …$150.00 – 175.00

Higgins & Seiter
FLORENTINE
Whiskey tumblers,
Doz. …$120.00 – 150.00
Pint Dec. …$100.00 – 125.00
Qt. …$125.00 – 150.00
Pt. Claret…$100.00 – 125.00
Qt. Claret…$125.00 – 150.00

T. B. Clark & Co.
PALMETTO
½ Gal. …$200.00 – 250.00

Higgins & Seiter
NAPOLEON
Each…$150.00 – 175.00

T. B. Clark & Co.
PALMETTO
Qt. …$125.00 – 150.00
3 Pt. …$175.00 – 200.00

Averbeck
ALABAMA
Pt. …$100.00 – 125.00
Qt. …$150.00 – 175.00

Averbeck
FLORIDA
(no handle)
Pt. …$125.00 – 150.00

Higgins & Seiter
GEORGIA
13"…$150.00 – 200.00

Higgins & Seiter
CUT STAR
Qt. Claret…$50.00 – 65.00
Pt. Claret…$75.00 – 90.00

DECANTERS AND JUGS

Higgins & Seiter
STRAWBERRY
DIAMOND FAN
Each…$125.00 – 150.00

T. B. Clark & Co.
ARBUTUS
with Sterling Top
Each…$175.00 – 200.00

T. B. Clark & Co.
CORAL
No handle…$150.00 – 175.00
Handle…$175.00 – 200.00

T. B. Clark & Co.
MANHATTAN
No handle…$125.00 – 15
Handle…$150.00 – 175.

Pitkins & Brooks
ORIOLE
P & B Grade
Qt. …$200.00 – 225.00

Pitkins & Brooks
SUNRAY
P & B Grade
Qt. …$150.00 – 175.00

T. B. Clark & Co.
PALMETTO
Flemish Jug
Each…$150.00 – 250.00
depending on size

T. B. Clark & Co.
DESDEMONA
Jug…$250.00 – 300.00

T. B. Clark & C0.
ARBUTUS
Wide mouth jug
½ Pt. …$100.00 – 125.00
Pt. …$125.00 – 150.00
Qt. …$150.00 – 175.00
3 Pt. …$175.00 – 250.00
½ Gal. …$200.00 – 250.00

Higgins & Seiter
CUT STAR
Each…$100.00 – 125.00

Pitkins & Brooks
AURORA BOREALIS
P & B Grade
1½ Pt. …$200.00 – 225.00

T. B. Clark & Co.
MANHATTAN
½ Pt. …$100.00 – 125.00
Pt. …$125.00 – 150.00
Qt. …$150.00 –175.00
3 Pt. …$175.00 200.00
½ Gal. …$200.00 – 250.00

FINGER BOWLS

J . D. Bergen
GOLF
4½"...$30.00 – 35.00
5"...$35.00 – 40.00

Averbeck
OCCIDENT
Each...$35.00 – 40.00

Averbeck
GEORGIA
Each...$35.00 – 40.00

J . D. Bergen
ELECTRIC
4½"...$30.00 – 35.00
5"...$35.00 – 40.00

Pitkins & Brooks
MARS
P & B Grade
Each...$30.00 – 35.00

Pitkins & Brooks
RAJAH
P & B Grade
Each...$40.00 – 45.00

Pitkins & Brooks
STANDARD
Each...$20.00 – 25.00

Pitkins & Brooks
Standard Grade
Each...$15.00 – 20.00

Pitkins & Brooks
BELMONT
P & B Grade
Each...$40.00 – 45.00

Pitkins & Brooks
IMPORTED
Each...$25.00 – 30.00

Pitkins & Brooks
BELMONT
P & B Grade
Each...$40.00 – 45.00

Higgins & Seiter
STRAWBERRY
DIAMOND FAN
Each...$35.00 – 40.00

J . D. Bergen
PREMIER
4½"...$30.00 – 35.00
5"...$40.00 – 45.00

Higgins & Seiter
NAPOLEON
Each...$25.00 – 30.00

Higgins & Seiter
FLORENCE
Each...$30.00 – 35.00

T. B. Clark & Co.
P. E.
Each...$30.00 – 35.00

T. B. Clark & Co.
WINOLA
Each...$30.00 – 35.00

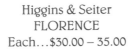

Higgins & Seiter
Each...$30.00 – 35.00

Higgins & Seiter
CUT STAR
Each...$20.00 – 25.00

Higgins & Seiter
SPECIAL FLORENTINE
Each...$25.00 – 30.00

T. B. Clark & Co.
WINOLA
Each...$35.00 – 40.00

GOBLETS

Averbeck
FLORIDA
$40.00 – 45.00

Pitkins & Brooks
SUNRISE
$10.00 – 12.00

Higgins & Seiter
CUT STAR
$18.00 – 20.00

Pitkins & Brooks
$30.00 – 35.00

Pitkins & Brooks
BELMONT
P & B Grade
$50.00 – 60.00

Averbeck
VIENNA
$40.00 – 50.00

Pitkins & Broc
HEART
P & B Grac
$50.00 – 60.

Higgins & Seiter
FLORENCE
$50.00 – 60.00

Pitkins & Brooks
MERLIN
$12.00 – 15.00

Higgins & Seiter
S/B DIAMOND FAN
$40.00 – 50.00

Pitkins & Brooks
Standard Grade
$30.00 – 35.00

J. D. Bergen
PREMIER
$35.00 – 40.00

Averbeck
ALABAMA
$40.00 – 50.00

Pitkins & Broo
Standard Grad
$25.00 – 30.0

Higgins & Seiter
DEWEY
$10.00 – 15.00

Averbeck
FLORIDA
$50.00 – 55.00

J. D. Bergen
ELECTRIC
$50.00 – 55.00

J. D. Bergen
ELECTRIC
$50.00 – 55.00

J. D. Bergen
GOLF
$50.00 – 55.00

Pitkins & Broc
$50.00 – 55.0

Pitkins & Brooks
$30.00 – 40.00

J. D. Bergen
MARIE
$50.00 – 55.00

Higgins & Seiter
FLORENTINE
$35.00 – 40.00

J. D. Bergen
MARIE
$50.00 – 60.00

Higgins & Seiter
$40.00 – 50.00

Averbeck
LIBERTY
$40.00 – 50.00

Averbeck
NAPLES
$40.00 – 50.00

74

GOBLETS

J. D. Bergen
ELECTRIC
$40.00 – 50.00

J. D. Bergen
GOLF
$40.00 – 50.00

J. D. Bergen
PREMIER
$50.00 – 60.00

J. D. Bergen
GOLF
$40.00 – 50.00

J. D. Bergen
PREMIER
$50.00 – 60.00

Pitkins & Brooks
VENICE
$40.00 – 50.00

Averbeck
ALABAMA
$40.00 – 50.00

J. D. Bergen
MARIE
$50.00 – 60.00

Averbeck
FLORIDA
$40.00 – 50.00

J. D. Bergen
PREMIER
$50.00 – 60.00

J. D. Bergen
ELECTRIC
$40.00 – 50.00

Pitkins & Brooks
SUNRISE
$10.00 – 12.00

J. D. Bergen
ELECTRIC
$40.00 – 50.00

J. D. Bergen
PREMIER
$40.00 – 50.00

Pitkins & Brooks
HEART
P & B GRADE
$60.00 – 70.00

Averbeck
RADIUM
$40.00 – 50.00

J. D. Bergen
ELECTRIC
$40.00 – 50.00

Pitkins & Brooks
$10.00 – 12.00

Pitkins & Brooks
$10.00 – 12.00

Pitkins & Brooks
$10.00 – 12.00

Pitkins & Brooks
$25.00 – 30.00

Averbeck
FLORIDA
$40.00 – 50.00

Pitkins & Brooks
Standard Grade
$25.00 – 30.00

Averbeck
ALABAMA
$40.00 – 50.00

Averbeck
PRISCILLA
$40.00 – 50.00

GOBLETS

Averbeck FLORIDA $40.00 – 50.00	J. D. Bergen GOLF $40.00 – 50.00	Averbeck FLORIDA $40.00 – 50.00	Averbeck ALABAMA $40.00 – 50.00	J. D. Bergen ELECTRIC $40.00 – 50.00	Pitkins & Brooks VENICE $40.00 – 45.00

Pitkins & Brooks SUNRISE $10.00 – 12.00	Pitkins & Brooks P & B Grade $60.00 – 70.00	J. D. Bergen GOLF $40.00 – 50.00	Averbeck FLORIDA $40.00 – 50.00	J. D. Bergen PREMIER $40.00 – 50.00	Averbeck RUBY $40.00 – 50.00

Averbeck GEORGIA $40.00 – 50.00	T. B. Clark & Co. WINOLA $35.00 – 40.00	T. B. Clark & Co. WINOLA 35.00 – 40.00	J. D. Bergen ELECTRIC $40.00 – 50.00	J. D. Bergen MARIE $50.00 – 60.00	Averbeck ALABAMA $40.00 – 50.00

Pitkins & Brooks BELMONT P & B Grade $40.00 – 50.00	Pitkins & Brooks $40.00 – 50.00 $30.00 – 40.00	Pitkins & Brooks $10.00 – 12.00 $30.00 – 40.00	Pitkins & Brooks $40.00 – 50.00	Pitkins & Brooks $40.00 – 50.00 $40.00 – 50.00	Pitkins & Bro $10.00 – 12.0

ICE CREAM

Pitkins & Brooks
Ice Cream Tray
Standard Grade
15"…$400.00 – 500.00

Pitkins & Brooks
MERLIN
Footed Sherbet
Each…$20.00 – 25.00

Pitkins & Brooks
Ice Cream Saucer
Standard Grade
6"…$75.00 – 90.00

J. D. Bergen
MILDRED
Footed Sherbet
Each…$75.00 – 90.00

Averbeck
RENAISSANCE
Ice Cream Tray
8" x 12"…$50.00 – 65.00

Higgins & Seiter
WEBSTER
Ice Cream Saucer
5" or 6"…$40.00 – 50.00

Higgins & Seiter
WASHINGTON
6"…$40.00 – 50.00

Pitkins & Brooks
OAK LEAF
Ice Cream Saucer
P & B Grade
6"…$75.00 – 90.00

Pitkins & Brooks
OAK LEAF
Ice Cream Tray
P & B Grade
13"…$400.00 – 450.00

ICE CREAM TRAYS

Averbeck
RUBY
Ice Cream Tray
14"...$200.00 – 250.00

Averbeck
VIENNA
Ice Cream Tray
14"...$250.00 – 300.00

Averbeck
FRISCO
Ice Cream Tray
14"...$250.00 – 300.00

T. B. Clark & Co.
WINOLA
Ice Cream Tray
Each...$250.00 – 300.00

T. B. Clark & Co.
VENUS
Ice Cream Tray
Each...$400.00 – 450.00

T. B. Clark & Co.
ADONIS
Ice Cream Tray
Each...$400.00 – 450.00

T. B. Clark & Co.
MANHATTAN
Ice Cream Tray
Each...$350.00 – 400.00

ICE CREAM TRAYS

Higgins & Seiter
ARLINGTON
Ice Cream Tray
8½" x 13½" …$200.00 – 250.00

Higgins & Seiter
WEBSTER
Ice Cream Tray
8½" x 14"…$300.00 – 350.00

J. D. Bergen
PROGRESS
Ice Cream Tray
18" x 10½"…$500.00 – 600.00
14" x 8"…$400.00 – 500.00

J. D. Bergen
FRISCO
Ice Cream Tray
10½" x 18"…$500.00 – 550.00

J. D. Bergen
SEYMOUR
10" x 16"…$500.00 – 600.00

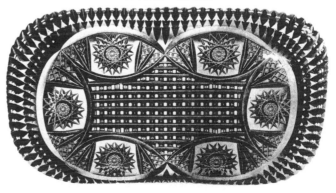

J. D. Bergen
KENWOOD
9" x 16"…$400.00 – 450.00

ICE CREAM TRAYS

J. D. Bergen
RAJAH
8" x 14½"...$400.00 – 450.00

J. D. Bergen
ARABIAN
10" x 16"...$400.00 – 500.00

AZALIA
9" dia. ...$200.00 – 250.00
12" dia. ...$350.00 – 400.00
14" dia. ...$400.00 – 450.00

J. D. Bergen
PUTNAM
9" x 16"...$500.00 – 600.00

J. D. Bergen
EAGLE
11" x 17"...$400.00 – 500.00

ICE TUBS

J. D. Bergen
GLENWOOD
Plate & Drainer
6" x 6½"…$250.00 – 300.00

J. D. Bergen
FLORIDA
Tub & Plate
5¾" x 7¾"…$300.00 – 350.00

J. D. Bergen
GOLF
7"…$150.00 – 200.00

Higgins & Seiter
BELVEDERE
Footed
5" x 9"…$200.00 – 225.00

J. D. Bergen
AMAZON
4¾" x 7"…$200.00 – 250.00

Higgins & Seiter
ADMIRAL
4" x 6"…$150.00 – 175.00

J. D. Bergen
IVANHOE
Tub with Drainer
Each…$250.00 – 300.00

T. B. Clark & Co.
CORAL
Tub & Plate
Each…$250.00 – 300.00

Higgins & Seiter
THE ESTELLE
4¾" x 4"…$125.00 – 150.00

Higgins & Seiter
NAPOLEON
Tub & Plate
Each…$250.00 – 300.00

Higgins & Seiter
WEBSTER
4" x 4½"…$125.00 – 150.00

Higgins & Seiter
ARLINGTON
Tub with Drainer
7" x 4¼"…$125.00 – 150.00

ICE TUBS

T. B. Clark & Co.
JEWEL
Each…$200.00 – 250.00

Averbeck
IVY
10" x 5"…$200.00 – 250.00

Averbeck
RADIUM
3¾" High…$150.00 – 175.00

Averbeck
MAUD ADAMS
6" x 9"…$200.00 – 225.00

MISCELLANEOUS BOWLS

Pitkins & Brooks
SPARKLE
Nut Bowl
Standard Grade
6"…$75.00 – 90.00

Pitkins & Brooks
AERO NUT BOWL
P & B Grade
5½"…$90.00 – 100.00

Pitkins & Brooks
ST. REGIS
Nut Bowl
P & B Grade
5½"…$90.00 – 100.00

Pitkins & Brooks
STAR
Whipped Cream
Standard Grade
7"…$90.00 – 110.00

Averbeck
LIBERTY
Whipped Cream
7" x 4½"…$75.00 – 100.00

Pitkins & Brooks
SAVANNAH MELON
P & B Grade
7½"…$100.00 – 125.00

JEWEL BOXES AND HAIR RECEIVERS

Pitkins & Brooks
DELMAR
Jewel Box
P & B Grade
7"...$125.00 – 150.00

Pitkins & Brooks
HIAWATHA
Jewel Box
P & B Grade
Each...$125.00 – 150.00

Pitkins & Brooks
MERRIMAC
Jewel Box
P & B Grade
6"...$150.00 – 175.00

Pitkins & Brooks
SPARKLE
Jewel Box
P & B Grade
7"...$175.00 – 200.00

J. D. Bergen & Co.
OAKLAND
Jewel Case
3½" x 4"...$125.00 – 150.00

Pitkins & Brooks
ELECTRA
Hair Receiver
Each...$125.00 – 150.00

Pitkins & Brooks
AURORA BOREALIS
Hair Receiver
P & B Grade
5"...$75.00 – 100.00

Pitkins & Brooks
HIAWATHA
Hair Receiver
P & B Grade
5"...$100.00 – 125.00

Pitkins & Brooks
ALADDIN
Hair Receiver
P & B Grade
4½"...$125.00 – 150.00

Pitkins & Brooks
LAROSE
Hair Receiver
P & B Grade
5"...$125.00 – 150.00

Pitkins & Brooks
ESTHER
Hair Receiver
P & B Grade
5"...$125.00 – 150.00

Pitkins & Brooks
ASTER
Hair Receiver
Standard Grade
5½"...$100.00 – 125.00

LAMPS

Pitkins & Brooks
CHRYSANTHEMUM
Electric Lamp, Engraved
P & B Grade
with 32 prisms
17"...$1,000.00 – 1,250.00

Pitkins & Brooks
DELMAR ELECTRIC
Rock Crystal Effect
P & B Grade
with or without prisms
17"...$1,000.00 – 1,250.00

Pitkins & Brooks
POPPY
Electric Lamp, Engraved
P & B Grade
with prisms
22"...$1,250.00 – 1,500.00

Pitkins & Brooks
ARC
Electric Lamp
& Shade
P & B Grade
12½"...$350.00 – 450.00

Higgins & Seiter
CHRYSANTHEMUM
23"...$1,000.00 – 1,200.00

Higgins & Seiter
RICH CUT GLASS
21"...$600.00 – 750.00

LAMPS

Pitkins & Brooks
ELECTRA ELECTRIC
P & B Grade
26"...$1,500.00 – 2,000.00

Pitkins & Brooks
ORO
Electric Lamp
& Shade
P & B Grade
14"...$1,200.00 – 1,500.00

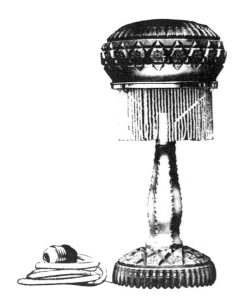

Pitkins & Brooks
AURORA BOREALIS
Electric Lamp
P & B Grade
12½" x 6"...$650.00 – 800.00

Pitkins & Brooks
DELMAR ELECTRIC
P & B Grade
with prisms
14" ...$650.00 – 800.00

J. D. Bergen
KENWOOD
Silver-plated Mountings
& Fount
22"...$1,500.00 – 2,000.00

J. D. Bergen
PREMIER
14½"...$550.00 – 750.00
22"...$750.00 – 1,000.00

Pitkins & Brooks
DAISY ELECTRIC
Engraved
P & B Grade
32 prisms
17"...$1,200.00 – 1,500.00

Pitkins & Brooks
PANSY ELECTRIC
Engraved
P & B Grade
32 prisms
17"...$1,200.00 – 1,500.00

MISCELLANEOUS TABLEWARE

T. B. Clark & Co.
HENRY VIII
Sugar Sifter
with sterling top
Each…$125.00 – 150.00

Pitkins & Brooks
TOPAZ
Grapefruit
P & B Grade
7½" across top…$100.00 – 125.00

T. B. Clark & Co.
HENRY VIII
Tea Caddy
with sterling top
Each…$125.00 – 150.00

Pitkins & Brooks
PRISM MAYONNAISE
Bowl & Plate
P & B Grade
6"…$100.00 – 125.00

Pitkins & Brooks
MAYONNAISE BOWL
Standard Grade
5" across top…$70.00 – 80.00

Averbeck
SARATOGA
Napkin Ring
Each…$30.00 – 35.00

Pitkins & Brooks
OLIVE JAR
Imported
6½"…$25.00 – 30.00

T. B. Clark & Co.
HENRY VIII
Syrup Jug
Plated Top
Small size…$125.00 – 150.00
Large size…$150.00 – 200.00

Pitkins & Brooks
BORDER NUT BOWL
P & B Grade
8"…$150.00 – 200.00

Pitkins & Brooks
PLAZA MAYONNAISE
Boat & Tray
P & B Grade
Pair…$250.00 – 300.00

T. B. Clark & Co.
JEWEL
Pepper Sauce Bottle
Sterling top…$100.00 – 125.00

MISCELLANEOUS TABLEWARE

J. D. Bergen
GOLF
Horseradish
6"...$100.00 – 125.00

Higgins & Seiter
Horseradish Jar
H & S
5¼"...$75.00 – 90.00

J. D. Bergen
SAVOY
Horseradish Jar
Each...$100.00 – 125.00

Higgins & Seiter
NAPOLEON
Horseradish Jar
5¼"...$75.00 – 90.00

J. D. Bergen
ELECTRIC
Horseradish Jar
Each...$100.00 – 125.0

Higgins & Seiter
RENAISSANCE
Horseradish Jar
5¼"...$40.00

Pitkins & Brooks
DELMAR
Worcestershire
Bottle
P & B Grade
8"...$100.00 – 125.00

Pitkins & Brooks
IMPORTED
Horseradish
Each...$20.00 – 22.00

Higgins & Seiter
STRAWBERRY & FAN CUTTING
Worcestershire
Bottle
8"...$100.00 – 125.00

Higgins & Seiter
STRAWBERRY & FAN C
Horseradish Jar
5¼"...$75.00 – 90.

Higgins & Seiter
Mustard or Horseradish Jars
Each...$20.00 – 22.00

Higgins & Seiter
NAPOLEON
Mustard or Horseradish Jars
Each...$50.00 – 65.00

Higgins & Seiter
RENAISSANCE
Horseradish or Mustar
Each...$35.00 – 50.00

Higgins & Seiter
STRAWBERRY
DIAMOND & FAN
Catsup Bottle
7"...$75.00 – 90.00

Higgins & Seiter
STRAWBERRY
DIAMOND & FAN
Tabasco Sauce Bottle
7"...$100.00 – 125.00

Pitkins & Brooks
DELMAR
Tabasco Bottle
P & B Grade
Each...$100.00 – 125.00

Higgins & Seiter
MAJESTIC
Worcestershire Bottle
Each...$100.00 – 125.00

Higgins & Seiter
7"...$75.00 – 90.00

MISCELLANEOUS

Pitkins & Brooks
HIAWATHA FERN
Dish & Liner
P & B Grade
8"…$75.00 – 90.00

Pitkins & Brooks
TOPAZ CLOCK
P & B Grade
5½"…$250.00 – 350.00

Higgins & Seiter
Cigar Cutter & Ash
Receiver Cut Glass
Sterling Silver
4"…$75.00 – 90.00

Averbeck
PRISM
Loving Cup
½ Pt. …$30.00 – 50.00

Pitkins & Brooks
MURONO
Ashtray
P & B Grade
3½" to 5½"…$30.00 – 45.00

Pitkins & Brooks
CURIO DISH
P & B Grade
9"…$90.00 – 125.00

Averbeck
PAPERWEIGHT
Each…$50.00 – 65.00

Averbeck
LONDON
Oval Bowl or Dish
12"…$150.00 – 175.00

J. D. Bergen
GIRARD
Fancy Tray or
Cake Plate
6½" x 14"…$300.00 – 350.00

Pitkins & Brooks
DON CARD CASE
P & B Grade
4"…$30.00 – 35.00

Pitkins & Brooks
VIVIAN
Hat Pin Holder
P & B Grade
7"…$75.00 – 90.00

J. D. Bergen
MADONNA
Cake or Bread Tray
11½" x 7"…$200.00 – 250.00

PICKLE DISHES AND OLIVE TRAYS

Averbeck
MARIETTA
Pickle Dish
8"…$75.00 – 90.00

Averbeck
SARATOGA
Pickle Dish
8"…$65.00 – 80.00

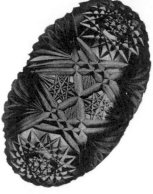

Averbeck
RUBY
Pickle Dish
8"…$75.00 – 90.00

Averbeck
ROYAL
Pickle Dish
8"…$90.00 –110.00

Averbeck
CANTON
Pickle Dish
8"…$100.00 – 125.00

Averbeck
EMPRESS
Pickle Dish
8"…$100.00 – 125.00

Averbeck
SARATOGA
Olive Dish
7¼"…$75.00 – 90.00

Averbeck
MARIETTA
Olive Dish
7¾"…$100.00 – 125.00

Averbeck
LADY CURZON
Olive Dish
7¾"…$75.00 – 90.00

Pitkins & Brooks
NELLORE PICKLE
P & B Grade
7"…$75.00 – 90.00

Averbeck
CANTON
7¾"…$100.00 – 125.00

Pitkins & Brooks
MEADVILLE PICKLE
Standard Grade
7"…$75.00 – 90.00

Averbeck
RUBY
Olive Dish
7¾"…$75.00 – 90.00

Averbeck
PRISCILLA
Olive Dish
7¾"…$75.00 – 90.00

PITCHERS AND TANKARDS

Averbeck
FLORIDA
2 Pt. Water
10½"...$150.00 – 175.00

Averbeck
NAPLES
4 Pt. Water
10½"...$200.00 – 225.00

Averbeck
GEORGIA
3 Pt. Jug
9¾" x 7½"...$175.00 – 200.00

J. D. Bergen
GOLDENROD
2 Qt. Pitcher
Each...$200.00 – 250.00

Higgins & Seiter
LAKELAND
Claret Pitcher
Sterling-Silver Mounted
1 Qt. ...$150.00 – 175.00
3 Pts. ...$200.00 – 225.00

J. D. Bergen
DELTA
½" Pt. ...$125.00 – 140.00
1 Pt. ...$140.00 – 160.00
1 Qt. ...$160.00 – 175.00
2 Qt. ...$175.00 – 200.00

PITCHERS AND TANKARDS

Higgins & Seiter
SYROTT
Claret Pitcher
1 Qt. ...$150.00 – 200.00
3 Pt. ...$200.00 – 250.00

Averbeck
NICE
2 Pt. ...$200.00 – 250.00

Higgins & Seiter
MAINE
Claret Pitcher
1Qt. ...$150.00 – 175.00
2 Pt. ...$200.00 – 225.00

Higgins & Seiter
NAPOLEON
1 Pt. ...$150.00 – 175.00
1 Qt. ...$175.00 – 200.00
2 Pt. ...$200.00 – 250.00

Higgins & Seiter
S/B DIAMOND FAN
Tankard Jug
⅓ Pt. ...$100.00 – 125.00
½ Pt. ...$125.00 – 150.00
1 Pt. ...$150.00 – 175.00
1 Qt. ...$175.00 – 200.00
3 Qt. ...$200.00 – 225.00

Higgins & Seiter
S/B DIAMOND FAN
Tankard Jug
½ Pt. ...$80.00 – 100.00
1 Pt. ...$90.00 – 110.00
1 Qt. ...$95.00 – 115.00
3 Pt. ...$125.00 – 150.00
2 Qt. ...$150.00 – 175.00

Higgins & Seiter
LAKELAND
Claret Jug
11"...$200.00 – 250.00

Higgins & Seiter
S/B DIAMOND FAN
Tankard Jug
1 Qt. ...$50.00 – 60.00
2½ Pt. ...$50.00 – 60.00
3 Pt. ...$60.00 – 75.00
2 Qt. ...$60.00 – 75.00

PITCHERS AND TANKARDS

Pitkins & Brooks
STANDARD JUG
3 Pt. ...$125.00 – 150.00

J. D. Bergen
ALLYN
1 Qt. ...$150.00 – 175.00
2 Qt. ...$175.00 – 200.00

Averbeck
RUBY
2 Pt. ...$125.00 – 150.00

J. D. Bergen
GOLF
Claret
2 Qt. ...$200.00 – 250.00

Pitkins & Brooks
ORLEANS JUG
P & B Grade
4 Pt. ...$175.00 – 200.00

J. D. Bergen
PERSIAN
Claret Jug
3 Pt. ...$250.00 – 300.00

J. D. Bergen
PREMIER
Claret Jug
2 Qt. ...$250.00 – 300.00

PITCHERS AND TANKARDS

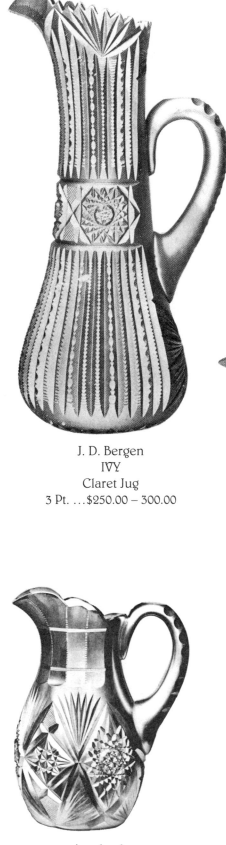

Averbeck
GENOA
Water
3 Pt. ...$200.00 – 250.00

J. D. Bergen
ELECTRIC
Claret Jug
2 Qt. ...$200.00 – 250.00

J. D. Bergen
IVY
Claret Jug
3 Pt. ...$250.00 – 300.00

Averbeck
VIENNA
3 Pt. ...$150.00 – 200.00

J. D. Bergen
PRINCETON
Claret Jug
3 Pt. ...$300.00 – 350.00

Averbeck
TRIXY
2 Pt. ...$150.00 – 175.00
3 Pt. ...$175.00 – 200.00

PITCHERS AND TANKARDS

Averbeck
FLORIDA
2 Pt. . . .$150.00 – 175.00
3 Pt. . . .$175.00 – 200.00

J. D. Bergen
PREMIER
Claret Jug
3 Pt. . . .$300.00 – 350.00

Averbeck
SARATOGA
4 Pt. . . .$175.00 – 200.00

Averbeck
VIENNA
2 Pt. . . .$150.00 – 175.00
3 Pt. . . .$200.00 – 250.00

Averbeck
GENOA
4 Pt. . . .$225.00 – 250.00

Averbeck
ALABAMA
2 Pt. . . .$125.00 – 150.00
3 Pt. . . .$175.00 – 200.00

Pitkins & Brooks
KELZ JUG
Standard Grade
3 Pt. . . .$100.00 – 150.00

Averbeck
MAUD ADAMS
4 Pt. . . .$225.00 – 250.00

PITCHERS AND TANKARDS

J. D. Bergen
BEDFORD
1 Qt. ...$175.00 – 200.00
2 Qt. ...$200.00 – 250.00

J. D. Bergen
ETHEL
1 Qt. ...$175.00 – 200.00
2 Qt. ...$200.00 – 250.00

J. D. Bergen
DALLAS
2 Qt. ...$300.00 – 350.00

J. D. Bergen
GOLF
½ Pt. ...$100.00 – 125.00
1 Pt. ...$125.00 – 150.00
1 Qt. ...$150.00 – 175.00
2 Qt. ...$200.00 – 250.00

Averbeck
VIENNA
3 Pt. ...$200.00 – 225.00

Higgins & Seiter
AMAZON
Cut Glass with Sterling
Silver hand-chased
mounting.
2 Pt. ...$150.00 – 175.00
3 Pt. ...$200.00 – 225.00

Averbeck
GEORGIA
1 Pt. ...$100.00 – 150.00

PITCHERS AND TANKARDS

J. D. Bergen
MARIE
2 QT. ...$300.00 – 350.00

J. D. Bergen
COLONY
2 QT. ...$300.00 – 350.00

J. D. Bergen
PREMIER
1 Qt. ...$175.00 – 200.00
2 Qt. ...$200.00 – 250.00

J. D. Bergen
EVANS
1 Qt. ...$150.00 – 175.00
2 Qt. ...$175.00 – 200.00

Higgins & Seiter
OTIS
2 Qt. ...$200.00 – 225.00
1 Qt. ...$150.00 – 175.00

Higgins & Seiter
DEWEY
2 Qt. ...$200.00 – 225.00
1 Qt. ...$150.00 – 175.00

Averbeck
RUBY
2 Pt. ...$150.00 – 175.00
3 Pt. ...$175.00 – 200.00

PITCHERS AND TANKARDS

J. D. Bergen
GOLF
1 Qt. ...$150.00 – 175.00
2 Qt. ...$175.00 – 200.00

J. D. Bergen
WILLARD
1 Qt. ...$150.00 – 175.00
2 Qt. ...$200.00 – 225.00

J. D. Bergen
FEDERAL
2 Qt. ...$250.00 – 300.00

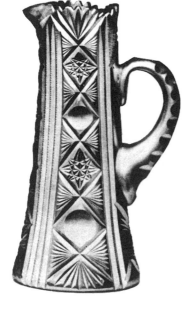

Averbeck
RUBY
3 Pt. ...$200.00 – 225.00

Pitkins & Brooks
ORLEANS JUG
P & B Grade
3 Pt. ...$200.00 – 225.00

PLATEAUS

Pitkins & Brooks
MOUNTED
Silver-plated
Standard Grade
10"...$25.00 – 35.00
12"...$35.00 – 45.00
14"...$45.00 – 55.00
16"...$55.00 – 65.00
18"...$65.00 – 75.00

Pitkins & Brooks
MOUNTED PLATEAU
Silver-plated
Standard Grade
10"...$25.00 – 35.00
12"...$35.00 – 45.00
14"...$45.00 – 55.00
16"...$55.00 – 65.00
18"...$65.00 – 75.00

Pitkins & Brooks
HANDLED TRAY
Silver-plated
Standard Grade
12"...$30.00 – 35.00
14"...$35.00 – 40.00
16"...$40.00 – 45.00

Pitkins & Brooks
MOUNTED PLATEAU
Silver-plated
Standard Grade
8"...$20.00 – 25.00
10"...$25.00 – 30.00
12"...$30.00 – 35.00
14"...$35.00 – 40.00

Pitkins & Brooks
MOUNTED PLATEAU
Silver-plated
Standard Grade
10"...$25.00 – 35.00
12"...$35.00 – 45.00
14"...$45.00 – 55.00

Pitkins & Brooks
MOUNTED PLATEAU
Silver-plated
Standard Grade
10"...$20.00   25.00
12"...$25.00 – 30.00
14"...$30.00 – 35.00
16"...$35.00 – 40.00

PLATEAUS

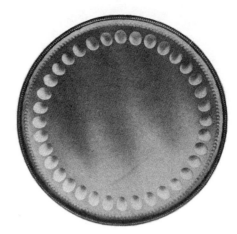

Pitkins & Brooks
BEADED PLATEAU
Standard Grade
8"...$10.00 – 12.00
10"...$15.00 – 20.00
12"...$20.00 – 25.00
14"...$25.00 – 30.00
16"...$30.00 – 35.00
18"...$35.00 – 40.00

Pitkins & Brooks
CONCAVE
& BEADED
Standard Grade
8"...$15.00 – 20.00
10"...$20.00 – 25.00
12"...$25.00 – 30.00
14"...$30.00 – 35.00

Pitkins & Brooks
Standard Grade
10"...$20.00 – 25.00
12"...$25.00 – 30.00
14"...$30.00 – 35.00
16"...$35.00 – 40.00

Pitkins & Brooks
STAR PLATEAU
Standard Grade
8"...$15.00 – 20.00
10"...$20.00 – 25.00
12"...$25.00 – 30.00
14"...$30.00 – 35.00
16"...$35.00 – 40.00
18"...$40.00 – 45.00

Pitkins & Brooks
Standard Grade
10"...$20.00 – 25.00
12"...$25.00 – 30.00
16"...$35.00 – 40.00
18"...$40.00 – 45.00

PLATES AND SAUCERS

Pitkins & Brooks
KENWOOD
5" Sau. ...$50.00 – 60.00
6" Sau. ...$60.00 – 70.00

Averbeck
BOSTON
7" Plate...$50.00 – 60.00

Averbeck
LOWELL
7" Plate...$70.00 – 80.00

J. D. Bergen
WEBSTER
5" Sau. ...$50.00 – 60.00
6" Sau. ...$60.00 – 70.00

J. D. Bergen
BERMUDA
5" Sau. ...$50.00 – 60.00
6" Sau. ...$60.00 – 70.00

Pitkins & Brooks
ROLAND PLATE
P & B Grade
9" ...$100.00 – 125.00
12" ...$200.00 – 250.00
14" ...$300.00 – 350.00

J. D. Bergen
MAGNET
5" Sau. ...$50.00 – 60.00
6" Sau. ...$60.00 – 70.00

J. D. Bergen
CORSAIR
5" Sau. ...$50.00 – 60.00
6" Sau. ...$60.00 – 70.00

Averbeck
VIENNA
7" Plate ...$70.00 – 80.00

J. D. Bergen
GOLF
5" Sau. ...$50.00 – 60.00
6" Sau. ...$60.00 – 70.00

PLATES AND SAUCERS

J. D. Bergen
DELAWARE
9"...$200.00 – 250.00

J. D. Bergen
LAWTON
Fancy Dish
4-Lobed...$200.00 – 250.00

Averbeck
CAPE TOWN
7" Plate...$75.00 – 90.00

J. D. Bergen
ORIOLE
Fancy Dish
9"...$250.00 – 300.00

Averbeck
NEWPORT
7" Plate...$75.00 – 90.00

J. D. Bergen
BEDFORD
5" Sau. ...$50.00 – 60.00
6" Sau. ...$60.00 – 70.00

Averbeck
AMERICAN BEAUTY
7" Plate...$85.00 – 100.00

J. D. Bergen
ELECTRIC
7" Plate...$70.00 – 85.00

NAPPIES AND SAUCERS

Pitkins & Brooks
BERRIE NAPPY
P & B Grade
8"...$175.00 – 200.00

T. B. Clark & Co.
DESDEMONA
7"...$75.00 – 100.00
8"...$100.00 – 125.00
9"...$150.00 – 200.00
10"...$275.00 – 325.00

T. B. Clark & Co.
VENUS
8"...$125.00 – 175.00
9"...$200.00 – 250.00

T. B. Clark & Co.
VENUS
7-inch Round Plate
Each...$75.00 – 100.00

Higgins & Seiter
JUBILEE
6"...$40.00 – 50.00

T. B. Clark & Co.
ADONIS
9"...$150.00 – 200.00

Averbeck
GEM
5"...$25.00 – 35.00

Higgins & Seiter
WEBSTER
6"...$35.00 – 40.00

Averbeck
SARATOGA
7-inch Plate
Each...$75.00 – 90.00

105

T. B. Clark & Co.
WINOLA
5"...$40.00 – 50.00
6"...$50.00 – 60.00
7"...$75.00 – 100.00

T. B. Clark & Co.
ARBUTUS
7"...$60.00 – 75.00
8"...$75.00 – 95.00
9"...$95.00 – 120.00
10"...$125.00 – 150.00

T. B. Clark & Co.
MANHATTAN
5"...$40.00 – 50.00
6"...$50.00 – 65.00
7"...$75.00 – 100.00

Pitkins & Brooks
BEAVER SAUCER
Standard Grade
5"...$60.00 – 70.00
6"...$75.00 – 90.00

NAPPIES

Pitkins & Brooks
MIKADO HANDLED
Standard Grade
5"...$40.00 – 50.00
6"...$50.00 – 60.00

Pitkins & Brooks
MEADVILLE
Standard Grade
5"...$40.00 – 50.00
6"...$50.00 – 60.00

Pitkins & Brooks
VENICE
P & B Grade
5"...$40.00 – 50.00
6"...$50.00 – 60.00

Pitkins & Brooks
MARS
P & B Grade
5"...$40.00 – 50.00
6"...$60.00 – 75.00

Averbeck
DIAMOND
with handle:
5"...$40.00 – 50.00
6"...$60.00 – 70.00
without handle:
5"...$50.00 – 60.00
6"...$70.00 – 80.00

Averbeck
FRISCO
6"...$45.00 – 60.00

Averbeck
DIANA
with handle:
5"...$40.00 – 50.00
6"...$60.00 – 70.00
without handle:
5"...$50.00 – 60.00
6"...$70.00 – 80.00

Averbeck
MARIETTA
with handle:
5"...$40.00 – 50.00
6"...$60.00 – 70.00
without handle:
5"...$50.00 – 60.00
6"...$70.00 – 80.00

Averbeck
VIENNA
with handle:
5"...$40.00 – 50.00
6"...$60.00 – 70.00
without handle:
5"...$50.00 – 60.00
6"...$70.00 – 80.00

NAPPIES

J. D. Bergen
EMBLEM
5" Hld. …$50.00 – 60.00
6" Hld. …$70.00 – 80.00

J. D. Bergen
PROGRESS
5"…$50.00 – 60.00
6"…$70.00 – 80.00

J. D. Bergen
CORSAIR
5" Hld. …$45.00 – 55.00
6" Hld. …$65.00 – 75.00

J. D. Bergen
WEBSTER
5" Hld. …$50.00 – 60.00
6" Hld. …$70.00 – 80.00

J. D. Bergen
BEDFORD
5" Hld. …$50.00 – 60.00
6" Hld. …$70.00 – 80.00

J. D. Bergen
BERMUDA
5" Hld. …$45.00 – 55.00
6" Hld. …$65.00 – 75.00

Pitkins & Brooks
MYRTLE BERRY
Standard Grade
7"…$70.00 – 80.00
8"…$100.00 – 125.00

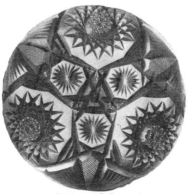

Pitkins & Brooks
CORSAIR BERRY
Standard Grade
7"…$70.00 – 80.00
8"…$100.00 – 125.00
9"…$150.00 – 175.00

Pitkins & Brooks
MEADVILLE BERRY
Standard Grade
7"…$100.00 – 125.00
8"…$100.00 – 125.00
9"…$150.00 – 175.00

NAPPIES

J. D. Bergen
GOLF
5" Hld. …$50.00 – 60.00
6" Hld. …$60.00 – 75.00

J. D. Bergen
WEBSTER
5" Hld. …$50.00 – 60.00
6" Hld. …$60.00 – 75.00

Pitkins & Brooks
MIKADO BERRY
Standard Grade
7"…$70.00 – 85.00

Averbeck
CAPE TOWN
7"…$75.00 – 90.00
8"…$90.00 – 110.00
9"…$150.00 – 185.00
10"…$200.00 – 225.00

Averbeck
CANTON
7"…$60.00 – 75.00
8"…$75.00 – 90.00
9"…$90.00 – 110.00
10"…$120.00 – 150.00

Averbeck
REGAL
7"…$75.00 – 90.00
8"…$90.00 – 110.00
9"…$150.00 – 185.00
10"…$200.00 – 225.00

Averbeck
RUBY
5" no Hld. …$65.00 – 75.00
6" no Hld. …$75.00 – 90.00
5" Hld. …$50.00 – 60.00
6" Hld. …$60.00 – 75.00

Averbeck
NAPLES
5" no Hld. …$65.00 – 80.00
6" no Hld. …$80.00 – 95.00
5" Hld.…$55.00 – 65.00
6" Hld. …$65.00 – 75.00

Averbeck
CANTON
5" no Hld. …$65.00 – 80.00
6" no Hld. …$80.00 – 95.00
5" Hld. …$55.00 – 65.00
6" Hld. …$65.00 – 75.00

Averbeck
LADY CURZON
5" no Hld. …$60.00 – 75.00
6" no Hld. …$75.00 – 90.00
5" Hld. …$50.00 – 60.00
6" Hld. …$60.00 – 70.00

NAPPIES

J. D. Bergen
AMBROSE
7"...$100.00 – 125.00
8"...$125.00 – 150.00
9"...$150.00 – 200.00
10"...$200.00 – 250.00

J. D. Bergen
CORSAIR
7"...$65.00 – 80.00
8"...$80.00 – 100.00
9"...$100.00 – 130.00
10"...$150.00 – 175.00

J. D. Bergen
KENWOOD
7"...$100.00 – 125.00
8"...$125.00 – 150.00
9"...$150.00 – 200.00

J. D. Bergen
BEDFORD
7"...$65.00 – 80.00
8"...$80.00 – 100.00
9"...$100.00 – 130.00
10"...$150.00 – 175.00

NAPPIES

Averbeck
RUBY
7"...$65.00 – 80.00
8"...$80.00 – 90.00
9"...$100.00 – 125.00
10"...$150.00 – 200.00

Averbeck
MARIETTA
7"...$65.00 – 75.00
8"...$75.00 – 90.00
9"...$90.00 – 110.00
10"...$125.00 – 150.00

Averbeck
OCCIDENT
7"...$100.00 – 125.00
8"...$150.00 – 175.00
9"...$200.00 – 225.00
10"...$250.00 – 300.00

Averbeck
PUCK
7"...$65.00 – 75.00
8"...$75.00 – 90.00
9"...$90.00 – 110.00
10"...$120.00 – 150.00

Averbeck
PARIS
7"...$65.00 – 80.00
8"...$80.00 – 90.00
9"...$100.00 – 125.00
10"...$150.00 – 200.00

Averbeck
FRISCO
7"...$60.00 – 75.00
8"...$75.00 – 90.00
9"...$90.00 – 110.00
10"...$120.00 – 150.00

Averbeck
SARATOGA
7"...$65.00 – 80.00
8"...$80.00 – 90.00
9"...$100.00 – 125.00
10"...$150.00 – 200.00

Averbeck
BRUSSELS
7"...$60.00 – 75.00
8"...$75.00 – 90.00
9"...$90.00 – 110.00
10"...$120.00 – 150.00

Averbeck
SPRUCE
7"...$60.00 – 75.00
8"...$75.00 – 90.00
9"...$90.00 – 110.00
10"...$120.00 – 150.00

NAPPIES

Averbeck
ACME
7"...$75.00 – 100.00
8"...$125.00 – 150.00
9"...$150.00 – 175.00
10"...$175.00 – 200.00

Averbeck
NEWPORT
5" no Hld. ...$60.00 – 75.00
6" no Hld. ...$75.00 – 90.00
5" Hld. ...$50.00 – 60.00
6" Hld. ...$60.00 – 75.00

Averbeck
AMERICAN BEAUTY
7"...$60.00 – 75.00
8"...$85.00 – 110.00
9"...$125.00 – 150.00
10"...$175.00 – 225.00

Averbeck
AMERICAN BEAUTY
5" no Hld. ...$65.00 – 80.00
6" no Hld. ...$80.00 – 95.00
5" Hld. ...$55.00 – 65.00
6" Hld. ...$65.00 – 75.00

Averbeck
LIBERTY
5" no Hld. ...$65.00 – 80.00
6" no Hld. ...$80.00 – 90.00
5" Hld. ...$55.00 – 65.00
6" Hld. ...$65.00 – 75.00

Averbeck
SPRUCE
5" no Hld. ...$60.00 – 75.00
6" no Hld. ...$75.00 – 90.00
5" Hld. ...$50.00 – 60.00
6" Hld. ...$60.00 – 75.00

Averbeck
HUDSON
5" no Hld. ...$60.00 – 75.00
6" no Hld. ...$75.00 – 90.00
5" Hld. ...$50.00 – 60.00
6" Hld. ...$60.00 – 75.00

T. B. Clark & Co.
DESDEMONA
Each...$150.00 – 175.00

Higgins & Seiter
ALASKA
5½"...$55.00 – 65.00

T. B. Clark & Co.
JEWEL
5"...$30.00 – 40.00
6"...$45.00 – 55.00
7"...$75.00 – 90.00

T. B. Clark & Co.
JEWEL
7"...$75.00 – 90.00
8"...$120.00 – 150.00
9"...$150.00 – 175.00
10"...$225.00 – 250.00

Higgins & Seiter
CLOVER
Leaf Shape
Each...$40.00 – 50.00

T. B. Clark & Co.
MANHATTAN
7"...$75.00 – 100.00
8"...$125.00 – 150.00
9"...$150.00 – 175.00
10"...$175.00 – 200.00

NAPPIES

J. D. Bergen
ST. LOUIS
7"…$65.00 – 80.00
8"…$80.00 – 100.00
9"…$100.00 – 130.00
10"…$150.00 – 175.00

J. D. Bergen
KENWOOD
7"…$100.00 – 120.00
8"…$125.00 – 150.00
9"…$150.00 – 200.00
10"…$200.00 – 250.00

J. D. Bergen
GOLDENROD
7"…$65.00 – 80.00
8"…$80.00 – 100.00
9"…$100.00 – 125.00
10"…$135.00 – 160.00

J. D. Bergen
RENWICK
7"…$100.00 – 125.00
8"…$125.00 – 150.00
9"…$150.00 – 200.00
10"…$200.00 – 250.00

J. D. Bergen
BERMUDA
7"…$65.00 – 80.00
8"…$80.00 – 100.00
9"…$100.00 – 125.00
10"…$135.00 – 160.00

J. D. Bergen
GOLF
7"…$65.00 – 80.00
8"…$80.00 – 90.00
9"…$90.00 – 110.00
10"…$125.00 – 150.00

Pitkins & Brooks
ORIOLE HANDLED
Standard Grade
5"…$35.00 – 40.00
6"…$40.00 – 50.00

J. D. Bergen
HAMPTON
7"…$100.00 – 125.00
8"…$125.00 – 150.00
9"…$150.00 – 200.00
10"…$200.00 – 250.00

J. D. Bergen
WEBSTER
7"…$65.00 – 80.00
8"…$80.00 – 100.00
9"…$100.00 – 130.00
10"…$150.00 – 175.00

PUFF BOXES AND GLOVE BOXES

Pitkins & Brooks
HEART PUFF BOX
P & B Grade
6"...$100.00 – 125.00

Pitkins & Brooks
TECK PUFF BOX
P & B Grade
5¼"...$100.00 – 125.00

Pitkins & Brooks
NORTHERN STAR
P & B Grade
6¾"...$125.00 – 150.00

Pitkins & Brooks
ESTHER PUFF BOX
P & B Grade
5"...$125.00 – 150.00

Pitkins & Brooks
ELECTRA PUFF BOX
P & B Grade
Each...$125.00 – 150.00

Pitkins & Brooks
GRACE PUFF BOX
P & B Grade
3½" to 5½" ...$100.00 – 125.00

Pitkins & Brooks
MABELLE PUFF BOX
P & B Grade
Each...$85.00 – 100.00

Pitkins & Brooks
ASTER PUFF BOX
Standard Grade
5"...$100.00 – 125.00

Pitkins & Brooks
CRETE PUFF BOX
P & B Grade
Each...$125.00 – 150.00

Pitkins & Brooks
DELMAR GLOVE BOX
P & B Grade
11"...$220.00 – 250.00

Pitkins & Brooks
HIAWATHA GLOVE BOX
P & B Grade
10½"...$180.00 – 200.00

PUNCH BOWLS

Pitkins & Brooks
RAJAH
P & B Grade
Footed
10"...$500.00 – 600.00

Pitkins & Brooks
HEART
P & B Grade
12"...$750.00 – 900.00
14"...$1,000.00 – 1,250.00

Pitkins & Brooks
BEVERLY FOOTED
P & B Grade
12"...$650.00 – 800.00
14"...$900.00 – 1,200.00

J. D. Bergen
MARLOW
Low Footed
12"...$600.00 – 750.00

PUNCH BOWLS

Pitkins & Brooks
CRETE
P & B Grade,Footed
10"...$450.00 – 600.00
12"...$750.00 – 900.00

T. B. Clark & Co.
DESDEMONA
14"...$450.00 – 550.00

T. B. Clark & Co.
CORAL
14"...$1,000.00 – 1,250.00
12"...$750.00 – 1,000.00

T. B. Clark & Co.
ARBUTUS
14"...$325.00 – 400.00

Higgins & Seiter
WEBSTER
Each...$350.00 – 400.00

J. D. Bergen
CORSAIR
14"...$350.00 – 400.00

PUNCH BOWLS

Pitkins & Brooks
SUNBURST
P & B Grade
12"...$500.00 – 750.00

Pitkins & Brooks
CAROLYN
P & B Grade
14"...$900.00 – 1,200.00

Pitkins & Brooks
CAROLYN
P & B Grade
12"...$600.00 – 750.00

PUNCH BOWLS

Pitkins & Brooks
BELMONT
P & B Grade
14"...$1,000.00 – 1,200.00

Pitkins & Brooks
GARLAND
P & B Grade
12"...$750.00 – 900.00

Pitkins & Brooks
PLYMONTH
P & B Grade
12"...$850.00 – 1,000.00
14"...$1,250.00 – 1,500.00

PUNCH BOWLS

J. D. Bergen
WABASH
14"...$1,250.00 – 1,500.00

T. B. Clark & Co.
DESDEMONA
14"...$1,500.00 – 1,750.00
12"...$900.00 – 1,200.00

Higgins & Seiter
LEADER
14"...$1,200.00 – 1,500.00

PUNCH BOWLS

J. D. Bergen
PEARL
14"...$1,500.00 – 1,750.00

Higgins & Seiter
BEDFORD
14"...$350.00 – 400.00

T. B. Clark & Co.
DESDEMONA
12"...$350.00 – 450.00

PUNCH BOWLS

J. D. Bergen
ELGIN
14"…$500.00 – 600.00

J. D. Bergen
ELSA
14"…$450.00 – 600.00

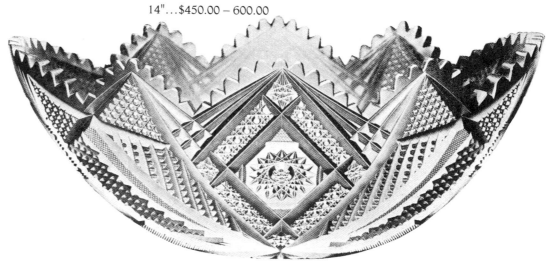

J. D. Bergen
ST. JAMES
15"…$750.00 – 900.00

PUNCH BOWLS

Pitkins & Brooks
KEYSTONE
P & B Grade
10"…$500.00 – 650.00
12"…$750.00 – 900.00
14"…$1,000.00 – 1,250.00

J. D. Bergen
MONTICELLO
12"…$650.00 – 800.00
14"…$1,200.00 – 1,500.00

Pitkins & Brooks
SUNRAY
Standard Grade
12"…$500.00 – 600.00

Pitkins & Brooks
DERBY
P & B Grade
12"…$600.00 – 750.00
14"…$900.00 – 1,100.00

PUNCH BOWLS

Averbeck
VIENNA
10"...$500.00 – 600.00
12"...$800.00 – 950.00
14"...$1,100.00 – 1,400.00

Averbeck
OCCIDENT
10"...$500.00 – 650.00
12"...$800.00 –1,000.00
14"...$1,250.00 – 1,500.00

J. D. Bergen
KENWOOD
12"...$750.00 – 900.00
14"...$1,200.00 – 1,500.00

J. D. Bergen
EDNA
14"...$1,200.00 – 1,500.00

J. D. Bergen
WABASH
Bowl and Stand…$1,200.00 – 1,500.00
Cups ea…$30.00 – 35.00
Ladle…$125.00 – 150.00
Plate…$40.00 – 50.00
Set…$1,800.00 – 2,200.00

PUNCH BOWLS

J. D. Bergen
PROGRESS
Bowl and Stand…$1,200.00 – 1,500.00
Cup ea. …$22.00 – 25.00
Set of cups (12)…$300.00 – 400.00
Ladle…$125.00 – 150.00
Plate…$40.00 – 50.00
Set…$2,00.00 – 2,500.00

J. D. Bergen
KENWOOD
Bowl…$1,200.00 – 1,500.00
Cup ea. …$40.00 – 50.00
Set of Cups (12)…$900.00 – 1,000.00
Ladle…$125.00 – 150.00
Plate…$40.00 – 50.00
Set…$2,500.00 – 3,000.00

PUNCH BOWLS

J. D. Bergen
GOLF
12"…$750.00 – 900.00
14"…$1,000.00 – 1,250.00

Higgins & Seiter
NAPOLEON
15"…$400.00 – 450.00

Higgins & Seiter
COMET
15"…$1,000.00 – 1,200.00

PUNCH BOWLS

J. D. Bergen
KENWOOD
Bowl…$1,200.00 – 1,500.00
Ladle…$125.00 – 150.00
Cup w/plates. …$40.00 – 50.00
Plateau…$40.00 – 50.00
Set (with 12 cups)…$2,500.00 – 3,000.00

SALT AND PEPPER SHAKERS

Pitkins & Brooks
$12.00 – 15.00

Pitkins & Brooks
$12.00 – 15.00

Pitkins & Brooks
$12.00 – 15.00

Pitkins & Brooks
$12.00 – 15.00

Pitkins & Brooks
$18.00 – 20.00

Pitkins & Brooks
Standard Grade
$12.00 – 15.00

itkins & Brooks
tandard Grade
$25.00 – 30.00

Pitkins & Brooks
Standard Grade
$12.00 – 15.00

Pitkins & Brooks
$22.00 – 25.00

Pitkins & Brooks
$22.00 – 25.00

Pitkins & Brooks
$25.00 – 30.00

J. D. Bergen
$25.00 – 30.00

Pitkins & Brooks
$25.00 – 30.00

Pitkins & Brooks
$25.00 – 30.00

J. D. Bergen
$30.00 – 35.00

J. D. Bergen
$25.00 – 30.00

Pitkins & Brooks
Standard Grade
$25.00 – 30.00

J. D. Bergen
$20.00 – 25.00

J. D. Bergen
$18.00 – 20.00

J. D. Bergen
$18.00 – 20.00

J. D. Bergen
$20.00 – 22.00

Pitkins & Brooks
$12.00 – 15.00

J. D. Bergen
$20.00 – 22.00

SALT AND PEPPERS SHAKERS

Pitkins & Brooks
$25.00 – 30.00

J. D. Bergen
$20.00 – 25.00

Pitkins & Brooks
Standard Grade
$25.00 – 30.00

Pitkins & Brooks
Standard Grade
$12.00 – 15.00

J. D. Bergen
$18.00 – 20.0

J. D. Bergen
$20.00 – 25.00

Pitkins & Brooks
$12.00 – 15.00

Pitkins & Brooks
$12.00 – 15.00

J. D. Bergen
$18.00 – 20.00

J. D. Bergen
$20.00 – 22.00

J. D. Bergen
$15.00 – 18.00

Pitkins & Brooks
$20.00 – 25.00

Pitkins & Brooks
$10.00 – 12.00

Pitkins & Brooks
$25.00 – 30.00

Pitkins & Broo
$10.00 – 12.00

J. D. Bergen
$30.00 – 35.00

Pitkins & Brooks
$12.00 – 15.00

J. D. Bergen
$30.00 – 35.00

Pitkins & Brooks
$12.00 – 15.00

Pitkins & Broo
$20.00 – 22.00

SALT AND PEPPER SHAKERS

J. D. Bergen
$12.00 – 15.00

Pitkins & Brooks
Standard Grade
$18.00 – 20.00

J. D. Bergen
$20.00 – 22.00

J. D. Bergen
$20.00 – 22.00

J. D. Bergen
$18.00 – 20.00

Pitkins & Brooks
$15.00 – 20.00

Pitkins & Brooks
$6.00 – 8.00

T. B. Clark & Co.
HENRY VIII
$20.00 – 25.00

Pitkins & Brooks
Standard Grade
$12.00 – 15.00

Pitkins & Brooks
Standard Grade
$10.00 – 12.00

Pitkins & Brooks
$15.00 – 18.00

Higgins & Seiter
$22.00 – 25.00

Pitkins & Brooks
$15.00 – 18.00

Higgins & Seiter
$15.00 – 18.00

Pitkins & Brooks
Standard Grade
$15.00 – 18.00

Higgins & Seiter
$15.00 – 18.00

Pitkins & Brooks
Standard Grade
$18.00 – 20.00

Pitkins & Brooks
Standard Grade
$25.00 – 30.00

Pitkins & Brooks
$15.00 – 18.00

Pitkins & Brooks
Standard Grade
$25.00 – 30.00

Pitkins & Brooks
$20.00 – 25.00

Pitkins & Brooks
Standard Grade
$15.00 – 18.00

Pitkins & Brooks
$20.00 – 22.00

Pitkins & Brooks
$6.00 – 8.00

J. D. Bergen
$20.00 – 25.00

SPOON DISHES AND SPOONERS

T. B. CLARK & Co.
JEWEL
Empress Spoon
Holder
Each…$100.00 – 125.00

Higgins & Seiter
WHEELER
Spoon Holder
Double Handled
Each…$125.00 – 130.00

Higgins & Seiter
FLORENCE
Spooner, Cut
Each…$100.00 – 125.00

Higgins & Seiter
NAPOLEON
Spooner
Each…$125.00 – 15

Averbeck
PRISM
Spooner
Each…$60.00 – 75.00

Averbeck
RUBY
Spooner
Each…$100.00 – 115.00

Averbeck
REGAL
Spooner
Each…$125.00 – 150.00

Higgins & Seiter
WEBSTER
Spooner
Each…$125.00 – 150

J. D. Bergen
AVON
Spooner
Each…$100.00 – 125.00

Averbeck
ASHLAND
Spooner
Each…$125.00 – 150.00

Averbeck
SARATOGA
Spooner
Each…$125.00 – 150.00

Pitkins & Brooks
TOOTHPICK HOLDE
2"…$20.00 – 22.00

TOOTHPICK HOLDERS

Pitkins & Brooks
2½"…$12.00 – 15.00

Pitkins & Brooks
TOOTHPICK HOLDER
2½"…$20.00 – 25.00

Pitkins & Brooks
TOOTHPICK HOLDER
2"…$20.00 – 25.00

Pitkins & Brooks
TOOTHPICK HOLDE
2"…$18.00 – 20.00

SPOON DISHES AND SPOONERS

Pitkins & Brooks
CORTEZ
P & B Grade
7½"…$75.00 – 90.00

Pitkins & Brooks
MEADVILLE
Standard Grade
7½"…$55.00 – 65.00

Pitkins & Brooks
VENICE
P & B Grade
Each…$75.00 – 90.00

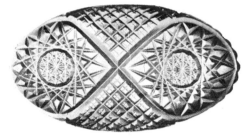

J. D. Bergen
BALTIC
Each…$75.00 – 85.00

Higgins & Seiter
CHRYSANTHEMUM
7¼"…$50.00 – 60.00

J. D. Bergen
OREGON
Each…$65.00 – 75.00

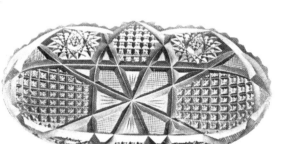

J. D. Bergen
TAMPA
Each…$65.00 – 80.00

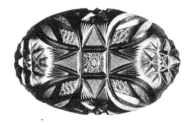

Averbeck
DIAMOND
Each…$50.00 – 65.00

Pitkins & Brooks
RAJAH
P & B Grade
Each…$100.00 – 125.00

T. B. Clark & Co.
MANHATTAN
Each…$50.00 – 60.00

Pitkins & Brooks
CRETE
P & B Grade
6½"…$60.00 – 75.00

Avereck
MARIETTA
Each…$75.00 – 90.00

Averbeck
NICE
Each…$75.00 – 90.00

Averbeck
VIENNA
Each…$75.00 – 90.00

131

SPOON DISHES AND SPOONERS

Averbeck MARIETTA	Averbeck NAPLES	Averbeck DIAMOND	Averbeck VIENNA
Each…$100.00 – 125.00	Each…$125.00 – 150.00	Each…$100.00 – 125.00	Each…$125.00 – 150.00

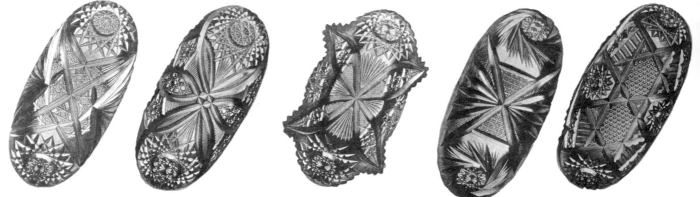

Averbeck CANTON	Averbeck EMPRESS	Averbeck MARIETTA	Averbeck SARATOGA	Averbeck DIANA
Each…$100.00 – 125.00	Each…$125.00 – 150.00	Each…$125.00 – 150.00	Each…$100.00 – 125.00	Each…$100.00 – 125.00

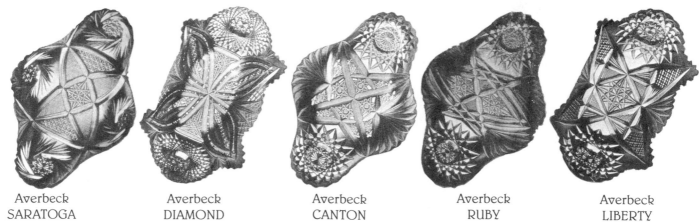

Averbeck SARATOGA	Averbeck DIAMOND	Averbeck CANTON	Averbeck RUBY	Averbeck LIBERTY
Each…$125.00 – 150.00	Each…$125.00 – 150.00	Each…$125.00 – 150.00	Each…$125.00 – 150.00	Each…$125.00 – 150.00

SPOONS, FORKS, AND LADELS

Averbeck
VIENNA
Punch Ladle
Each…$100.00 – 125.00

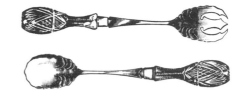

J. D. Bergen
Salad spoon w/Gorham
plate, cut glass handles
Spoon…$60.00 – 65.00
Spoons & Fork…$100.00 – 125.00

T. B. Clark & Co.
MANHATTAN
Salad Fork & Spoon
Pair…$75.00 – 100.00

J. D. Bergen
Punch ladle w/Gorham
sterling silver and cut
glass handle to match any
pattern.
16"…$125.00 – 150.00
14"…$100.00 – 125.00

T. B. Clark & Co.
DESDEMONA
Each…$100.00 – 125.00

J. D. Bergen
Salad fork, Gorham
Cut glass handles.
Fork only…$70.00 – 75.00
Fork & Spoon…$125.00 – 150.00

Higgins & Seiter
Silver-plated w/cut glass
handles.
Pair…$75.00 – 100.00
Solid silver, gold lined
$200.00 – 225.00

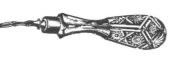

Higgins & Seiter
Silver-plated punch ladle,
cut glass handle.
Plated…$100.00 – 125.00
Solid silver…$125.00 – 150.00

J. D. Bergen
Salad set w/Gorham sterling,
cut glass handle.
Pair…$250.00 – 300.00

SYRUP AND MUSTARD HOLDERS

J. D. Bergen
PREMIER
Mustard & Plate
Set…$100.00 – 125.00

J. D. Bergen
PREMIER
Mustard
Each…$50.00 – 65.00

J. D. Bergen
Mustard
Each…$65.00 – 75.00

J. D. Bergen
OREGON
Half Pt. Syrup
Each…$125.00 – 150.00

Pitkins & Brooks
Mustard
Each…$50.00 – 65.00

J. D. Bergen
ELECTRIC
Half Pt. Syrup
Each…$125.00 – 150.00

J. D. Bergen
GLENWOOD
Half Pt. Syrup
Each…$125.00 – 150.00

Pitkins & Brooks
Mustard
Each…$50.00 – 65.00

J. D. Bergen
ELECTRIC
Half Pt. Syrup
Each…$125.00 – 150.00

TUMBLERS

T. B. Clark & Co.
$20.00 – 25.00

T. B. Clark & Co.
HENRY VIII
$30.00 – 35.00

T. B. Clark & Co.
CORAL
$30.00 – 35.00

T. B. Clark & Co.
MANHATTAN
$25.00 – 30.00

J. D. Bergen
GOLF
$30.00 – 35.00

Higgins & Seiter
$20.00 – 22.00

Pitkins & Brooks
$18.00 – 20.00

Pitkins & Brooks
WINFIELD
Standard Grade
$20.00 – 22.00

Pitkins & Brooks
$15.00 – 18.00

J.D. Bergen
WAVERLY
$25.00 – 30.00

Pitkins & Brooks
$15.00 – 18.00

Pitkins & Brooks
$15.00 – 18.00

Pitkins & Brooks
MARS
$20.00 – 25.00

Pitkins & Brooks
$15.00 – 18.00

Pitkins & Brooks
Standard Grade
$15.00 – 18.00

Pitkins & Brooks
$15.00 – 18.00

Pitkins & Brooks
$15.00 – 18.00

Pitkins & Brooks
$20.00 – 22.00

S/B DIAMOND FAN
$20.00 – 25.00

J. D. Bergen
ELECTRIC
$20.00 – 22.00

J. D. BERGEN
SAVOY
$20.00 – 22.00

Averbeck
MAUD ADAMS
$20.00 – 22.00

Pitkins & Brooks
NELLORE
Standard Grade
$20.00 – 22.00

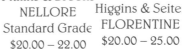

Higgins & Seiter
FLORENTINE
$20.00 – 25.00

Higgins & Seiter
FLORENTINE
$30.00 – 35.00

TUMBLERS

J. D. Bergen
PREMIER
½ Pt. ...$22.00 – 25.00
Champ...$30.00 – 35.00
Whiskey...$22.00 – 25.00

J. D. Bergen
ORIENT
½ Pt. ...$22.00 – 25.00
Champ...$30.00 – 35.00
Whiskey...$22.00 – 25.00

J. D. Bergen
GILMORE
½ Pt. ...$20.00 – 22.00
Champ...$25.00 – 30.00
Whiskey...$20.00 – 22.00

J. D. Bergen
NEWPORT
½ Pt. ...$22.00 – 25.00
Champ...$25.00 – 30.00
Whiskey...$20.00 – 22.00

J. D. Bergen
$18.00 – 20.00

J. D. Bergen
BEDFORD
$22.00 – 25.00

J. D. Bergen
05
$18.00 – 20.00

J. D. Bergen
03
$20.00 – 22.00

J. D. Bergen
07
$20.00 – 22.00

J. D. Bergen
COLONY
$22.00 – 25.00

J. D. Bergen
MARIE
$22.00 – 25.00

J. D. Bergen
DALLAS
$30.00 – 35.00

J. D. Bergen
PROGRESS
$30.00 – 35.00

J. D. Bergen
08
$18.00 – 20.00

T. B. Clark & Co.
WINOLA
$18.00 – 20.00

T. B. Clark & Co.
ARBUTUS
$22.00 – 25.00

T. B. Clark & Co.
JEWEL
$22.00 – 25.00

T. B. Clark & Co.
WINOLA
$18.00 – 20.00

TUMBLERS

Pitkins & Brooks
$10.00 – 12.00

Pitkins & Brooks
$18.00 – 20.00

Pitkins & Brooks
Standard Grade
$20.00 – 22.00

Pitkins & Brooks
Standard Grade
$20.00 – 22.00

Pitkins & Brooks
$10.00 – 12.00

Pitkins & Brooks
Standard Grade
$18.00 – 20.00

J. D. Bergen
ARLINGTON
$20.00 – 22.00

J. D. Bergen
EVANS
$20.00 – 22.00

J. D. Bergen
U. S.
$18.00 – 20.00

J. D. Bergen
GOLDENROD
$22.00 – 25.00

J. D. Bergen
NEWPORT
$22.00 – 25.00

J. D. Bergen
RESERVE
$15.00 – 18.00

J. D. Bergen
GOLF
$30.00 – 35.00

J. D. Bergen
ATLAS
$15.00 – 18.00

J. D. Bergen
ROLAND
$20.00 – 22.00

J. D. Bergen
BALTIMORE
$20.00 – 22.00

J. D. Bergen
ANSONIA
$22.00 – 25.00

J. D. Bergen
ETHEL
$22.00 – 25.00

J. D. Bergen
03
$20.00 – 22.00

J. D. Bergen
KNOX
$18.00 – 20.00

Pitkins & Brooks
$8.00 – 10.00

Pitkins & Brooks
$10.00 – 12.00

Higgins & Seiter
CUT STAR
$12.00 – 15.00

Higgins & Seiter
NAPOLEON
$22.00 – 25.00

T. B. Clark & Co.
WINOLA
$18.00 – 20.00

TUMBLERS

Averbeck
NICE
$25.00 – 30.00

Averbeck
SARATOGA
$22.00 – 25.00

Averbeck
ALABAMA
$22.00 – 25.00

Averbeck
RADIUM
$25.00 – 30.00

Averbeck
DAYTON
$22.00 – 25.00

Averbeck
BOSTON
$22.00 – 25.00

Averbeck
GENOA
$22.00 – 25.00

Averbeck
RUBY
$22.00 – 25.00

Averbeck
TRIXY
$20.00 – 22.00

Averbeck
ACME
$35.00 – 40.00

Averbeck
FLORIDA
$22.00 – 25.00

Averbeck
MAUD ADAMS
$20.00 – 22.00

Averbeck
LIBERTY
$22.00 – 25.00

Averbeck
RUBY
$22.00 – 25.00

Averbeck
MAINE
$22.00 – 25.00

Averbeck
MAUD ADAMS
22.00 – 25.00

Averbeck
VIENNA
$22.00 – 25.00

Averbeck
MELBA
$18.00 – 20.00

Averbeck
GEORGIA
$22.00 – 25.00

Averbeck
GENOA
$25.00 – 30.00

Averbeck
LIBERTY
$22.00 – 25.00

Averbeck
TRIXY
$20.00 – 22.00

Averbeck
GENOA
$22.00 – 25.00

Averbeck
VIENNA
$22.00 – 25.00

Averbeck
MELBA
$18.00 – 20.00

Averbeck
FLORIDA
$22.00 – 25.00

Averbeck
LIBERTY
$22.00 – 25.00

VASES

Pitkins & Brooks
P & B Grade
11"...$100.00 – 110.00
12½"...$125.00 – 150.00
14"...$150.00 – 175.00

J. D. Bergen
TROPHY
6"...$30.00 – 40.00
8"...$40.00 – 60.00
10"...$60.00 – 80.00
12"...$80.00 – 100.00
14"...$135.00 – 150.00

J. D. Bergen
DIXON
8"...$150.00 – 200.00
10"...$200.00 – 300.00
12"...$300.00 – 400.00
14"...$400.00 – 500.00

Averbeck
NICE
12"...$350.00 – 450.00
15"...$600.00 – 800.00
18"...$800.00 – 1,000.00

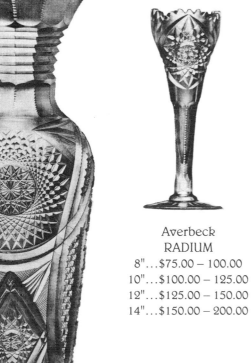

Averbeck
RADIUM
8"...$75.00 – 100.00
10"...$100.00 – 125.00
12"...$125.00 – 150.00
14"...$150.00 – 200.00

Averbeck
LIBERTY
8"...$75.00 – 100.00
10"...$100.00 – 125.00
12"...$125.00 – 150.00
14"...$150.00 – 200.00

Averbeck
NAPLES
17"...$600.00 – 750.00

Averbeck
SARATOGA
14"...$400.00 – 500.00

VASES

Pitkins & Brooks
STAR VASE
P & B Grade
10"…$250.00 – 350.00
13"…$400.00 – 500.00
16"…$600.00 – 750.00

J. D. Bergen
SUNBEAM
21"…$2,500.00 – 3,500.00
(two pieces)

J. D. Bergen
RUTLAND
6"…$60.00 – 75.00
8"…$100.00 – 115.00
10"…$150.00 – 175.00
12"…$175.00 – 200.00
14"…$200.00 – 225.00

VASES

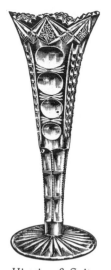

Higgins & Seiter
FLORENTINE
8"…$65.00 – 75.00
10"…$90.00 – 100.00
12"…$100.00 – 115.00
14"…$150.00 – 175.00
16"…$175.00 – 200.00

Pitkins & Brooks
8"…$100.00 – 125.00
9"…$125.00 – 150.00
10"…$150.00 – 175.00
12"…$200.00 – 250.00

Averbeck
DAISY
8"…$75.00 – 100.00
10"…$100.00 – 125.00
12"…$125.00 – 150.00
14"…$150.00 – 200.00

Higgins & Seiter
EVERETT
8"…$65.00 – 75.00
10"…$90.00 – 100.00
12"…$100.00 – 115.00
14"…$150.00 – 175.00
16"…$175.00 – 200.00

Higgins & Seiter
INDIA
12"…$300.00 – 350.00

T. B. Clark & Co.
PALMETTO
7"…$750.00 – 100.00
8"…$100.00 – 125.00
10"…$125.00 – 150.00
12"…$175.00 – 200.00
15"…$200.00 – 250.00
18"…$350.00 – 450.00

VASES

T. B. Clark & Co.
HEROIC
Each…$90.00 – 100.00

T. B. Clark & Co.
ORIENT
9"…$150.00 – 175.00
12"…$200.00 – 250.00

T. B. Clark & Co.
PALMETTO
Lg. …$150.00 – 175.00
Sm. …$125.00 – 150.00

Higgins & Seiter
B9/602
9"…$125.00 – 150.00
10"…$175.00 – 200.00
12"…$200.00 – 250.00

Higgins & Seiter
FLORENTINE
8"…$125.00 – 150.00
10"…$150.00 – 175.00
12"…$200.00 – 250.00

T. B. Clark & Co.
ADONIS
15"…$250.00 – 300.00
18"…$300.00 – 400.00

Pitkins & Brooks
P & B Grade
12½"…$200.00 – 250.00

Averbeck
ALABAMA
6"…$50.00 – 65.00
8"…$85.00 – 100.00
12"…$150.00 – 175.00
14"…$200.00 – 250.00

Averbeck
PRISM
8"…$125.00 – 150.00

T. B. Clark & Co.
HENRY VIII
7"…$75.00 – 100.00
8"…$100.00 – 125.00
10"…$125.00 – 150.00
12"…$175.00 – 225.00
15"…$250.00 – 300.00

Pitkins & Brooks
BELMONT BUD
P & B Grade
Each…$95.00 – 110.00

Higgins & Seiter
NAPOLEON
4½"…$75.00 – 85.00

142

VASES

Pitkins & Brooks
ROSABELLA
Standard Grade
8"…$100.00 – 125.00
10"…$150.00 – 200.00
12"…$200.00 – 250.00

Averbeck
ASHLAND
6"…$50.00 – 65.00
8"…$85.00 – 100.00
10"…$100.00 – 125.00
12"…$150.00 – 175.00
14"…$200.00 – 250.00

Pitkins & Brooks
Each…$50.00 – 75.00

Pitkins & Brooks
P & B Grade
10½"…$200.00 – 250.00

Pitkins & Brooks
HIAWATHA SWEET
PEA
P & B Grade
8"…$175.00 – 200.00

Pitkins & Brooks
ARANS
P & B Grade
10"…$150.00 – 200.00
12"…$250.00 – 300.00
14"…$300.00 – 350.00

Pitkins & Brooks
TECK VASE
P & B Grade
10"…$100.00 – 150.00
12"…$150.00 – 200.00

Pitkins & Brooks
ARANS
P & B Grade
14"…$200.00 – 250.00

Pitkins & Brooks
EYES
P & B Grade
12"…$125.00 – 150.00

Averbeck
DIAMOND
12"…$250.00 – $300.00

Averbeck
RUBY
Each…$150.00 – 200.00

T. B. Clark & Co.
HENRY VIII
7"…$75.00 – 100.00
9"…$150.00 – 200.00
12"…$200.00 – 250.00

Averbeck
FLORIDA
6"…$65.00 – 75.00
8"…$90.00 – 100.00
10"…$100.00 – 115.00
12"…$150.00 – 175.00
14"…$175.00 – 200.00

VASES

J. D. Bergen
NEVADA
8"…$175.00 – 200.00
10"…$200.00 – 250.00
12"…$250.00 – 300.00

J. D. Bergen
FAUST
6"…$100.00 – 125.00
7"…$125.00 – 150.00
8"…$150.00 – 200.00
9"…$200.00 – 250.00

Pitkins & Brooks
AURORA BOREALIS
P & B Grade
6½"…$175.00 – 200.00

Averbeck
ASHLAND
5"…$75.00 – 90.00

Averbeck
LIBERTY
Each…$100.00 – 175.00

T. B. Clark & Co.
WINOLA
Each…$75.00 – 90.00

T. B. Clark & Co.
DESDEMONA
Each…$250.00 – 300.00

T. B. Clark & Co.
4"…$75.00 – 100.00
6"…$100.00 – 125.00

Averbeck
MELBA
4"…$60.00 – 75.00

Averbeck
ASHLAND
4"…$60.00 – 75.00

J. D. Bergen
ELECTRIC
3-Handled Rose Ball
3½"…$45.00 – 60.00

T. B. Clark & Co.
MANHATTAN
6"…$100.00 –125.00
7"…$125.00 – 150.00
8"…$150.00 – 200.00

Averbeck
FLORIDA
5"…$75.00 – 100.00
6"…$100.00 – 125.00
7"…$125.00 – 150.00

J. D. Bergen
PREMIER
3½"…$45.00 – 50.00
4½"…$50.00 – 60.00
6"…$100.00 – 125.00
7"…$125.00 – 150.00
8"…$150.00 – 200.00
9"…$200.00 – 250.00

Pitkins & Brook
VIOLET BUD VAS
P & B Grade
5"…$75.00 – 90.0

VASES

J. D. Bergen
GOLDENROD
3"…$50.00 – 60.00
4"…$60.00 – 75.00
5"…$75.00 – 90.00
6"…$100.00 – 125.00

J. D. Bergen
CLIFTON
9"…$150.00 – 200.00
12"…$200.00 – 250.00
15"…$300.00 – 350.00

J. D. Bergen
NEVADA
3"…$50.00 – 65.00
4"…$75.00 – 90.00
6"…$100.00 – 125.00

Averbeck
GENOA
10"…$300.00 – 350.00

Averbeck
PRISCILLA
Each…$60.00 – 75.00

Averbeck
GENOA
2- Handled
12"…$300.00 – 400.00

J. D. Bergen
GOLDENROD
7"…$125.00 –150.00
8"…$150.00 – 200.00
10"…$200.00 – 250.00
12"…$250.00 – 300.00

Pitkins & Brooks
AMANDA
P & B Grade
10"…$150.00 – 200.00
12"…$200.00 – 250.00
14"…$250.00 – 300.00

Pitkins & Brooks
GLEE VASE
P & B Grade
8"…$250.00 – 300.00

VASES

Averbeck
MELBA
6"…$65.00 – 75.00
8"…$90.00 – 100.00
10"…$100.00 – 115.00
12"…$150.00 –175.00
14"…$175.00 – 200.00

J. D. Bergen
UNITY
9"…$250.00 – 300.00
12"…$300.00 – 350.00
15"…$400.00 – 500.00

J. D. Bergen
SHELDON
8"…$150.00 – 200.00
10"…$200.00 – 300.00
12"…$300.00 – 400.00
14"…$400.00 – 500.00

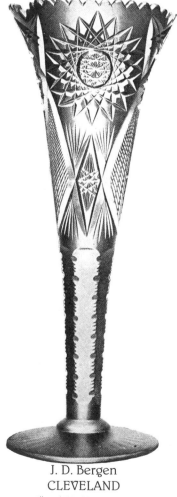

Pitkins & Brooks
ROSE VASE
P & B Grade
8"…$200.00 – 250.00

Averbeck
VIENNA
8"…$150.00 – 200.00
10"…$200.00 – 250.00
12"…$250.00 – 300.00

J. D. Bergen
CLEVELAND
6"…$50.00 – 65.00
8"…$75.00 – 90.00
10"…$100.00 – 125.00
12"…$150.00 – 175.00
14"…$175.00 – 200.00

Pitkins & Brooks
BERRIE FLOWER
HOLDER
P & B Grade
8"…$200.00 – 250.00

VASES

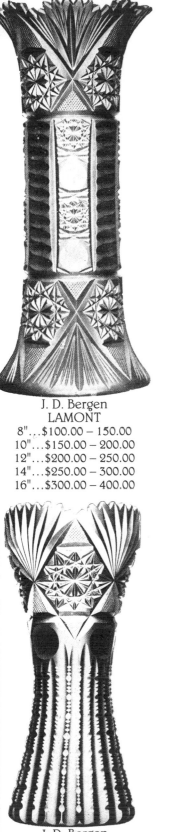

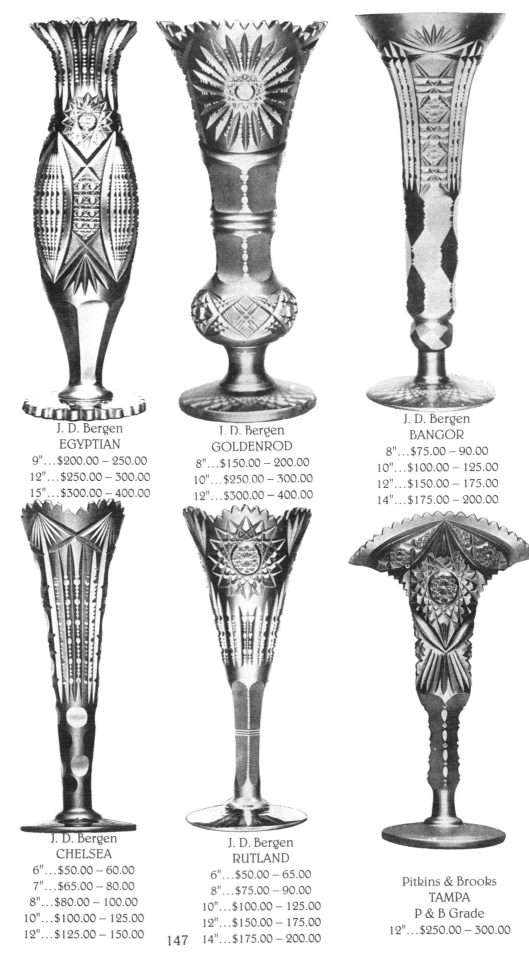

J. D. Bergen
LAMONT
8"...$100.00 – 150.00
10"...$150.00 – 200.00
12"...$200.00 – 250.00
14"...$250.00 – 300.00
16"...$300.00 – 400.00

J. D. Bergen
EGYPTIAN
9"...$200.00 – 250.00
12"...$250.00 – 300.00
15"...$300.00 – 400.00

I. D. Bergen
GOLDENROD
8"...$150.00 – 200.00
10"...$250.00 – 300.00
12"...$300.00 – 400.00

J. D. Bergen
BANGOR
8"...$75.00 – 90.00
10"...$100.00 – 125.00
12"...$150.00 – 175.00
14"...$175.00 – 200.00

J. D. Bergen
BELMORE
6"...$90.00 – 110.00
8"...$100.00 – 150.00
10"...$150.00 – 175.00
12"...$175.00 – 225.00
14"...$225.00 – 275.00

J. D. Bergen
CHELSEA
6"...$50.00 – 60.00
7"...$65.00 – 80.00
8"...$80.00 – 100.00
10"...$100.00 – 125.00
12"...$125.00 – 150.00

J. D. Bergen
RUTLAND
6"...$50.00 – 65.00
8"...$75.00 – 90.00
10"...$100.00 – 125.00
12"...$150.00 – 175.00
14"...$175.00 – 200.00

Pitkins & Brooks
TAMPA
P & B Grade
12"...$250.00 – 300.00

VASES

Pitkins & Brooks
P & B Grade
10"…$100.00 – 125.00

J. D. Bergen
COLONY
9"…$200.00 – 250.00
12"…$350.00 – 450.00

J. D. Bergen
KENWOOD
12"…$350.00 – 400.00
15"…$450.00 – 600.00
18"…$600.00 – 750.00

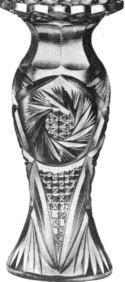

Averbeck
ROME
11"…$200.00 – 225.00

J. D. Bergen
CALUMET
9"…$200.00 – 250.00
12"…$300.00 – 350.00
15"…$400.00 – 450.00

Pitkins & Brooks
TOKA
P & B Grade
10"…$125.00 – 150.00
12"…$150.00 – 200.00
15"…$200.00 – 250.00

Pitkins & Brooks
CHRISTIANA VASE
Standard Grade
8"…$100.00 – 125.00
10"…$125.00 – 150.00
12"…$150.00 – 200.00
14"…$200.00 – 250.00

VASES

Pitkins & Brooks
Each…$65.00 – 100.00

Pitkins & Brooks
DIAMOND
P & B Grade
11"…$200.00 – 250.00

Pitkins & Brooks
P & B Grade
8"…$100.00 – 125.00
10"…$150.00 – 175.00
13"…$175.00 – 200.00
15"…$200.00 – 250.00
18"…$300.00 – 400.00
20"…$400.00 – 500.00

Pitkins & Brooks
FORGET-ME-NOT
Vase, Engraved
P & B Grade
12"…$250.00 – 300.00

Pitkins & Brooks
TRUSELLA VASE
P & B Grade
10"…$200.00 – 250.00

Pitkins & Brooks
ELECTRIC VASE
P & B Grade
10"…$200.00 – 250.00
12"…$250.00 – 300.00
14"…$300.00 – 350.00
16"…$400.00 – 450.00

Pitkins & Brooks
BERRIE
P & B Grade
14"…$200.00 – 250.00
18"…$300.00 – 350.00

Pitkins & Brooks
WALDORF
P & B Grade
10"…$150.00 – 175.00
12"…$175.00 – 200.00
14"…$200.00 – 225.00
16"…$250.00 – 300.00
18"…$300.00 – 400.00

Pitkins & Brooks
TECK VASE
P & B Grade
9½"…$250.00 – 300.00

Pitkins & Brooks
ORLEANS VASE
P & B Grade
11"…$200.00 – 250.00

Pitkins & Brooks
WALDORF
P & B Grade
8½"…$200.00 – 250.00

VASES

J. D. Bergen
RIALTO
12"...$300.00 – 400.00
14"...$400.00 – 500.00

J. D. Bergen
QUEEN
10"...$150.00 – 175.00
12"...$200.00 – 225.00
14"...$250.00 – 300.00

J. D. Bergen
LYDA
9"...$100.00 – 150.00
12"...$175.00 – 225.00
15"...$250.00 – 300.00

J. D. Bergen
UTAH
4"...$100.00 – 125.00
6"...$150.00 – 175.00
8"...$200.00 – 250.00

J. D. Bergen
NUTWOOD
4"...$100.00 – 125.00
6"...$150.00 – 175.00
8"...$200.00 – 250.00

J. D. Bergen
CORA
6"...$50.00 – 65.00
8"...$75.00 – 90.00
10"...$100.00 – 125.00
12"...$150.00 – 175.00
14"...$175.00 – 200.00

VASES

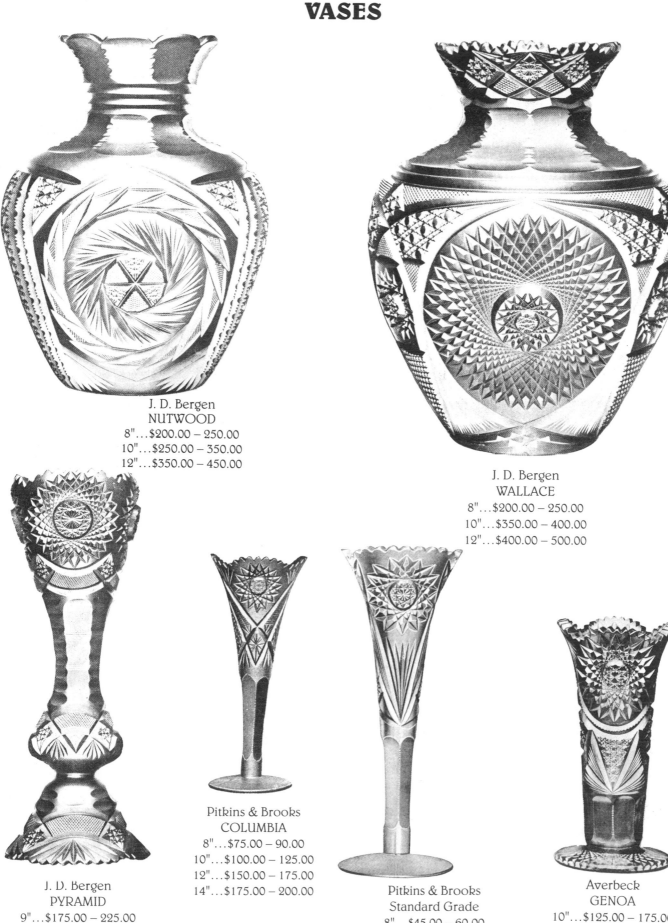

J. D. Bergen
NUTWOOD
8"...$200.00 – 250.00
10"...$250.00 – 350.00
12"...$350.00 – 450.00

J. D. Bergen
WALLACE
8"...$200.00 – 250.00
10"...$350.00 – 400.00
12"...$400.00 – 500.00

J. D. Bergen
PYRAMID
9"...$175.00 – 225.00
10"...$250.00 – 350.00
15"...$350.00 – 450.00

Pitkins & Brooks
COLUMBIA
8"...$75.00 – 90.00
10"...$100.00 – 125.00
12"...$150.00 – 175.00
14"...$175.00 – 200.00

Pitkins & Brooks
Standard Grade
8"...$45.00 – 60.00
10"...$65.00 – 70.00
12"...$75.00 – 80.00
14"...$85.00 – 110.00

Averbeck
GENOA
10"...$125.00 – 175.00
12"...$175.00 – 225.00
14"...$250.00 – 350.00

WATER SETS

J. D. Bergen
NEWPORT
Set…$250.00 – 300.00

J. D. Bergen
BEDFORD
Set…$330.00 – 375.00

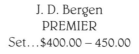

J. D. Bergen
BOSTON/ATLAS
Set…$225.00 – 250.00

J. D. Bergen
PREMIER
Set…$400.00 – 450.00

J. D. Bergen
ANSONIA
Set…$300.00 – 375.00

J. D. Bergen
GOLF
Set…$300.00 – 350.00

WATER SETS

Pitkins & Brooks
METROPOLE
8-Piece Water Set
Set...$350.00 – 400.00

Pitkins & Brooks
Standard Grade
8-Piece Water Set
Set...$250.00 – 350.00

Pitkins & Brooks
CARRIE
8-Piece Water Set
Set...$350.00 – 400.00

Pitkins & Brooks
CARLTON
8-Piece Water Set
Set...$300.00 – 350.00

Pitkins & Brooks
RUTH
8-Piece Water Set
Set...$400.00 – 450.00

WATER SETS

Pitkins & Brooks
CARNATION
8-Piece Water Set
Set…$350.00 – 400.00

Pitkins & Brooks
BERMUDA
8-Piece Water Set
Set…$400.00 – 500.00

J. D. Bergen
GOLF
Set…$450.00 – 500.00

INDEX

INDEX